A Marital
Therapy Manual

A Marital Therapy Manual

by

PETER A. MARTIN

JASON ARONSON INC.
Northvale, New Jersey
London

THE MASTER WORK SERIES

First softcover edition 1994

Library of Congress Cataloging-in-Publication Data

ISBN: 1-56821-171-6 (softcover)
Library of Congress Catalog Card Number 93-73985

Manufactured in the United States of America. Jason Aronson Inc. offers books and cassettes. For information and çatalog write to Jason Aronson Inc., 230 Livingston Street, Northvale, New Jersey 07647.

TO TILLIE

Commentary

"*A Marital Therapy Manual* is a valuable book for the psychotherapist and is worth reading for the introduction alone. Here the author places marital therapy in a well-earned pivotal position. In discussing the artificial boundaries between individual, family, and marital therapy Martin's viewpoint is consonant with the general systems approach, with which we will undoubtedly be increasingly occupied.

"Readers who have been put off by the extreme positions taken by some authors in the field of marital therapy will appreciate Martin's brief, readable clarification of the field as it relates to individual therapy. . . .

"A refreshing aspect of this work is the discussion of recurrent forces on the therapist as well as focus on the patient. Martin delineates problems as well as growth opportunities for the therapist; these, along with the innovations described, offer challenge and stimulation for the therapist feeling the need to enlarge his or her horizons."

—David Mendell, M.D.
American Journal of Psychiatry

Foreword

THIS BOOK occupies a unique position in psychological medicine. It is one of the first books in the history of American psychiatry that is devoted to marital therapy and designed for the benefit of those who are likewise engaged in the psychotherapy of patients presenting marital disharmony. Although intended as a clinician's handbook, it is much more.

It is a book that describes discoveries that have been woven into the psychotherapy of partners in marriage. Having been found repeatedly effective, they have become the techniques of an advanced form of marital therapy. The author's early discovery and use of the Stereoscopic Technique led to insights into marital disharmony that were analogous to the development of the electron microscope for molecular biology. These insights led to further development of new techniques through the years.

The value of this book for marital therapists is considerably enhanced by the author's description of four pathological marriage patterns commonly observed in the course of practice. The balancing of marital psychopathology with marital normality, of the diseased with the healthy, provides the marital therapist with the opportunity for developing a wholesome orientation instead of one that focuses only on sickness.

The values that comprise a healthy marriage pattern are also described in detail, and for the first time a psychologically healthy marriage pattern is described and becomes useful as a guide for marital therapists.

The new knowledge which characterizes this book is immediately available for translation into marital therapy. This is the author's hope and sole objective in writing this book—to share what he has learned with his colleagues. The same has been true of other great teachers of medicine.

This book is seen as a step in the further evolution of our knowledge and our humanistic efforts in behalf of those whose diseases are woven into the fabric of their marriages. It seems evident, moreover, that it reflects a new and more effective approach to the therapy of marital disharmony. The role of the marriage contract in the diagnosis and treatment is an example. In its masterly blending of theory and practice, this book may eventually become one of the foundations of a new specialty within the general framework of psychotherapy.

LEO H. BARTEMEIER, M.D.

Past President, American Psychiatric Association, American Psychoanalytic Association, and International Psychoanalytic Association

Contents

Preface

THIS BOOK IS A CLINICIAN'S HANDBOOK written for and about psychotherapists who will be or who are already involved in the treatment of marital problems. It is based on thirty years of experience as a psychoanalytic psychotherapist and twenty-five years of teaching and supervising psychotherapy of marital problems. It represents the techniques and principles that I have been teaching at several university and hospital training centers. The students have included (and it is to members of these groups that this book is addressed) medical students, family physicians, psychiatrists, clinical psychologists, psychiatric social workers, clergy, nurses, and marital and family therapists.

Intended as a practical, how-to-do-it handbook, this manual details a clinical approach derived from trial and error experiences and continuing clinical research during these three decades. It delineates the clinical entities found in the area of marital problems and describes many technical approaches that can be used to remedy the disorders. It is not about the sociological, anthropological, philosophical or moral aspects of marriage. Although it is impossible to do so completely, I have attempted to avoid polemics, value judgments, and proselytizing, so common in current literature, and not to involve the reader in the theoretical aspects of the many conflicting schools of psycho-

A MARITAL THERAPY MANUAL

therapy. Nor do I claim that one school of psychotherapy yields better results than any other. Although the approach I have developed is described, the literature of many other schools and methods is presented throughout.

I take this opportunity to give recognition and thanks to those who contributed to making this book possible. In the early years of my experimentation in this (at that time) unexplored field, Dr. Leo H. Bartemeier gave constant encouragement. I would also like to express my appreciation to those department of psychiatry chairmen who made possible, within university settings, the training and research on which this book is based. Dr. Raymond W. Waggoner, Sr., when Chairman of the Department of Psychiatry at the University of Michigan, facilitated the establishment of one of the first ongoing seminars on treatment of marriage problems for resident training. This innovation was established in 1967 in the face of the usual resistances and continues to function with the support of the current Chairman of the Department of Psychiatry, Dr. Albert J. Silverman. The cooperation of James F. McGloin, Jr., A.C.S.W., in organizing the seminars and in the preparation of this book has been extremely helpful. Dr. Jacques S. Gottlieb made facilities available at Wayne State University and Lafayette Clinic in Detroit for research into psychotherapeutic techniques for marital disharmony which added new dimensions to my experiences.

PETER A. MARTIN, M.D.

Southfield, Michigan
January 1976

A Marital
Therapy Manual

1

Introduction

SIMPLY PUT, A MARITAL THERAPIST is one who chooses to treat persons presenting marital problems. Beyond this, similarity between individual marital therapists often ends. There is no school with an acknowledged curriculum that trains such therapists as a separate profession. There is no unique theoretical base on which all marital therapy rests. Not only do marital therapists come from many disciplines, but even among those coming from the same discipline there are marked differences in goals and approaches to the same problems. I will avoid the term "marriage counselor," since marriage "counseling" frequently has an unfortunate and misleading connotation of being neither an important nor a depth-approach psychotherapy. Many do not realize that the variety and seriousness of the emotional problems encountered in disturbed marriages cover the entire range of diagnostic entities. In a survey of psychiatric residency training centers in the United States which examined (1) staff resistances to including marital and family therapy in core curriculum training and (2) residents' lack of clinical experience in treating marriage problems, depreciatory attitudes toward these treatment modalities were prominent among faculty and residents (Martin and Lief, 1973). They considered marital therapy to be "counseling" and counseling was regarded as short-term, superficial, and therefore not to be taken seriously by the already overloaded trainees who only had time for "what was important."

I will use the terms marital therapy and marital therapist exclusively because frequently the seriousness of the problems necessitates a corresponding depth therapy. The depth of the therapy in marital therapy is limited only by the training and the ability of the therapist. Some of the most difficult psychopathological problems that have failed to respond to dyadic therapy have been successfully treated by the advantageous conditions present in many types of marital therapy.

OVERLAPPING BOUNDARIES

Although the term "marital therapy" is a convenient catch-all phrase, which simplifies communication by linguistically limiting the area being studied, the field of marital therapy does not have sharply defined boundaries. For example, in 50 percent of cases of dyadic* therapy with a married person whose stated reason for entering therapy and whose symptomatology were apparently not related to the person's marriage, material emerges showing serious marital problems (Sager, et al., 1968). A psychotherapist must be capable of handling marital problems. When he does so in a dyadic setting, is this not marital therapy? Perhaps it should be called indirect marital therapy. Moreover, when material about children and family problems surfaces and is handled, is this not family therapy? In the historically famous case of Little Hans, Freud, working with the father and never seeing the young boy, resolved the child's phobia of horses (Freud, 1909). Perhaps this should be called indirect family therapy. Parenthetically, Freud may have been the first psychoanalytic marital therapist, although he never reported on his experience in the literature. Freud had in analysis, concurrently, both James and Alix Strachey, the husband and wife who became his English translators and publisher (Stone, 1971).

Just as the therapist doing dyadic therapy must handle marital and family problems, so the marital therapist cannot limit himself to the

---

* Since this is a therapist-oriented manual, the use of the term "dyadic therapy" in this book refers to the therapeutic dyad—one patient and one therapist.

interpersonal problems of the marriage. When intrapsychic problems of one of the mates prevents resolution of the marital disharmony, the marital therapist must be capable of applying himself to the task of individual therapy. In addition, the competent marital therapist cannot avoid dealing with presenting family problems. Likewise in doing family therapy, it may be necessary to deal with one individual's intrapsychic problem, as well as to handle a marital problem contributing to the family disorder.

It is clear that the fields of individual, marital, and family therapy have overlapping boundaries and that distinguishing one from the other is, to some extent, an artificial process. In fact, as any experienced, broadly trained psychotherapist knows, the following point is crucial: What is transpiring in any therapeutic setting is not determined by whether it is designated as individual, marital, or family therapy. It is determined by the needs of the patients and the capabilities, versatility, and training of the psychotherapist.

DISTINCTIVENESS OF MARITAL THERAPY

Marital therapy does, however, have some unique characteristics. It can deal with and effect changes in areas not possible in dyadic or family therapy. In contrast to family therapy, marital therapy can handle material of murderous hostilities and sexual disabilities between mates that cannot adequately be dealt with in the presence of children. Such material is traumatic to children, it can interfere with the natural sequence of their developmental stages and ego formation. The danger of the child's individuality being lost amidst florid actions of the adults helps to explain the observation that family therapy does not, as might be expected, follow naturally from child psychiatry. Child psychiatrists are oriented as child advocates. They often disagree with the "adulterers" who do marital therapy or family therapy and who try to help the children indirectly by resolving the parental pathogenic influences. Child therapists often prefer to stress that the child is an individual in his own right and does not merely react to what the parents are doing to him. They stress correctly that sometimes the child's individuality is the initiator of the parental distress. Child psychotherapists thus more readily recognize the separateness of marital therapy from the field of child psychiatry than do family therapists from their field.

Family therapy is distinctly different from marital therapy when children are present in the treatment room. Even then, however, family therapists seem more related to marital therapists than do child therapists. One of the most innovative of family therapists recently stated: "Although in particular situations I believe it is necessary to do *family* therapy throughout the course of treatment (i.e., including the children), I have moved more in the direction of working with the marriage relationship of the parents once the originally symptomatic children have become defocused. Most of my family therapy these days, then, becomes marital therapy" (Framo, 1975).

Perhaps the separateness of marital therapy is most clear when this type of treatment works in an area not possible in individual therapy. The intimacy and intensity of the marital bond often slows the therapeutic action of an individual's analysis and sometimes makes it impossible. Marital therapy brings the destructive bond into bold relief and, with both partners present, facilitates constructive changes. This advantage is best illustrated by recognition that many disturbed marriages are deeply rooted in a child-parent type of relationship. What Anna Freud said in her discussion of a paper on the simultaneous analysis of a mother and her adolescent daughter pertains to marital therapy: "Where the neurotic symptom, the conflict, or the regression of a child [read: *dependent mate*] is anchored not only in the young patient's [*dependent mate's*] own personality but held in place further by powerful emotional forces in the parent [*dominant mate*] to whom the child [*dependent mate*], in his turn, is tied, the therapeutic action of analysis may be slowed up or, in extreme cases, made imposible" (A. Freud, 1960).

Some therapists engaged in dyadic therapy do treat marital and family problems as more "grist for the mill" to be worked through in the treatment process. Others regard this material as interfering with the investigation of intrapsychic processes. Often mates and children are referred by them to another therapist to free the dyadic therapy from these interferences. Such referrals usually illustrate two different entities: one in which the original patients' complaints about their mates are realistic and individual progress is indeed blocked by the difficulties of the mate; the other in which the original patients used material of marital difficulty to avoid making intrapsychic changes. In dyadic therapy it is often difficult for the therapist to clarify which of these conditions obtains. In contrast, techniques of marital therapy allow for clarification of the issues involved. In those cases where the original patient's complaints are realistic, conjoint interviews can highlight the points of interaction between the abnormalities of the two mates. The original patient is not only anchored by his own anxieties and dependency but by powerful emotional forces in the mate that threatened frightening behavior, such as violence, suicidal attempts, emotional decompensation, desertion or divorce, so that continued analysis is made impossible. As in the bombing of London during World War II, the reality of the horrors of war precluded psychotherapy which focused on intrapsychic processes. In war-torn marriages, the dangerous milieu must be defused to allow the action of the original analysis to proceed. If the disturbing interpersonal relations are dealt with first, the intrapsychic problems then come back into focus.

All marriages involve a conscious and unconscious contract agreed upon before marriage and actively maintained by both partners throughout the balanced marriage. When one of the partners finds himself unable or unwilling to honor the original agreement, or when he has never intended to honor it and sets out to change the mate immediately after the marriage ceremony, marital disharmony occurs which is often manifested by symptom formation, conflict, or regression in the dependent partner. The following case strikingly illustrates these processes:

The husband was a confused, nonthinking, rule-following man married to a bright, dynamic, vivacious career-oriented woman. The unwritten contract that was understood and agreed upon between the two was that she could continue to pursue her personal interests without any interference from him. She could have a marriage and her career too, and he was to be grateful and feel lucky to have gotten her. This weak man, whose ego functioning was at times absent, looked to his wife to be his savior and his alter ego. She was more than willing to accept these roles, provided no questions were asked about her own activities. They maintained this relationship for several years until the husband developed severe panic reactions and entered analysis. He no longer could accept the contract to which he had tacitly agreed. It became clear that his panics were related to his wife. He had become very oppressive in his clinging attachment to her. The originally agreed upon relationship was not what he now wanted.

During his analysis, he had the following dream: "A man is swimming in shallow water—an odd, ludicrous figure. He is crawling around, not really swimming but going through the motions" (an obvious picture of his way of life). Then the patient sees himself in the kitchen, talking with his wife and her parents. They are supporting her position of being involved in her career activities outside the home. She states that she is going to continue to do whatever she wants to do. He goes upstairs, pouting. His wife follows him and says: "This is the only way I can make the marriage work. This is the only way I have a chance. If I stay home with you and the children, I will wither and dry up and become sick myself."

He awakened from this dream and thought: "No wonder she feels the way she does. I have been too gloomy, oppressive, self-centered, not aware of her needs." The marriage contract and neurosis are clear through his dream. In some of his unconscious fantasies, which became conscious during his analysis, a strong, powerful, successful man falls in love with his wife and, because of their relationship (which excludes sexual involvement), helps the patient and his wife make decisions and become financially successful. His unconscious was attuned to his wife's and vice-versa except for one item. She did become involved in extramarital sexual activities with powerful, successful men. He unconsciously realized this, resented it fiercely, but consciously denied her sexual involvements. He wanted her to love him as he loved her and to be sexually involved only with him. This material, rooted in the marital relationship, became a resistance to his analysis.

If he would become more adequate through his analytic work, his wife would work furiously to undermine his new position and reestablish the old relationship. This occurred in all areas, including the sexual one. When he had built himself up through his analysis to being especially adequate in sexual experiences and was very proud of his new-found prowess of bringing her to orgasm and having what he felt to be a great orgasm of his own, she responded typically. Instead of giving him the admiration, praise, and awe he had hoped for, she flipped him over so she was on top and, working furiously, had six tremendous orgasms of her own. During his relating of this story, one could almost hear the strains of the song, "I can do anything you can do, better," rising to exultant crescendos. His reaction to this experience was to become crestfallen and depressed. This is the position in which she wanted him to remain. She married him so that she could have the freedom of a one-sided open marriage, with the security of knowing that her husband would love her alone with a blind, unthinking devotion.

There was no way that he could be successful in his analysis without admitting to himself his wife's sexual involvement with other men, confronting her with it, and chancing the loss of his family. The wife refused any form of treatment. He terminated the analysis, leaving his "secret" knowledge and his wife unconfronted. As often happens, chance entered the picture. She found a powerful man, left her husband and children, and broke the marriage bond. He then could successfully complete his analysis. Change in his unconscious identification manifested itself in prowess in his field, becoming an excellent father, and making an entirely different type of marriage with a woman who respected and loved him. At this point, his ex-wife (whose second marriage had ended because the man was too powerful for her to tolerate), became enraged at him, claiming he had been dishonest and had not done what he had promised to do when they married.

In this example, the wife refused to enter any form of treatment. In other similar cases, the dominant mate accepts therapy and offers an opportunity to effect a change in the marriage contract. The change in the marital relationship then allows the original dependent mate to complete the work necessary for important intrapsychic changes. Ideally, the original analysis should have proceeded to where the man was capable of facing the reality of his wife and accepting the loss of his family. But this ideal is often defeated by such forces as economics, religion, ethnic attitudes, and attitudes about one's responsibilities to others. Effects of civilization do contribute to individual impotency in many patients. In clinical experience, it is often difficult for the individual in therapy to make such major changes because of the threatening reality. When such changes are made in dyadic therapy, it is usually done because it is the ego-strong, dominant mate who is in treatment and not the ego-weak, dependent mate. Such an ego-strong mate can make inner changes, carry the responsibility for maintaining the marital equilibrium or effect a separation, even if it involves the possibility of living with guilt feeling resulting from a suicide attempt by the dependent mate as a result of this change.

Some patients in dyadic therapy use complaints of marital difficulty to avoid intrapsychic changes. When these people are referred to a marital therapist, conjoint interviews often reveal that the original patients had been hiding their intrapsychic problems behind the screen of the interpersonal problems in the marriage. These patients' misrepresentation of the mates involves projective identifications that their therapists could not with certainty identify as such in dyadic interviews. In contrast, in the conjoint marital interviews, they found it difficult to hide their intrapsychic problems by complaining about the mates because of the reality of the mates' presence. Denial mechanisms are quickly and easily recognized. Such patients can then be returned to the original therapist for continuation of emphasis on intrapsychic changes.

Therapists who prefer to stress either the intrapsychic or the interpersonal aspects alone during therapy limit themselves. The opportunity is present for a greater sweep and scope and flexibility by moving back and forth from interpersonal to intrapsychic changes. In addition, the separation of intrapsychic from interpersonal and vice-versa is an artificial separation that does not occur in the nature of the human being. Intrapsychic phenomena and interpersonal phenomena are heads and tails of the same coin. Intrapsychic mechanisms determine the interpersonal relationship. The interpersonal relationship can perpetuate the intrapsychic phenomena by reinforcement or can effect an intrapsychic change as a result of new experience in the interpersonal relationship. Both vantage points are essential. They are complementary and neither should take precedence. At times the more relevant focus is intrapsychic and at other times it is interpersonal. The therapist should be capable of both views and should not stress one to the exclusion of the other.

EMPHASIS ON EFFECTING CHANGE

Marital therapy is not merely a short-term, superficial realignment of interpersonal conflict between relatively healthy mates. It involves a structured psychotherapeutic group that allows for intensive and extensive involvement in change, growth, and development. Many couples use a legitimate complaint of marital difficulty as an acceptable, face-saving way of receiving the help they seek as individuals. When this need is not recognized and help is not offered by the therapist, they are being deprived of a therapeutic right to treatment.

The seriousness of the problems encountered necessitates a corresponding depth of therapy. Such depth is possible in marital therapy. To emphasize again an important point, the depth of marital therapy is limited only by the training, versatility, and ability of the marital therapist. Some of the deepest and most difficult psychopathological problems which have failed to respond to dyadic therapy have been amenable to the conditions present in marital therapy that were not present in the dyadic therapy.

At one of the university centers where I have been conducting a continuing seminar on treatment of marriage problems, an unexpected development illustrated the depth and scope of marital therapy. After a few years of the seminar, it became apparent that a large percentage of marriages being referred for treatment involved at least one mate who had previously been hospitalized during a psychotic episode. After discharge from the acute episode, they had either been deemed unsuitable for psychotherapy, had been unable to use the psychotherapy made available (individual or group), or had found the drug therapy clinic regime insufficient to maintain their efforts at restitution In an attempt to get psychotherapy for them and to prevent rehospitalization, residents and parapsychiatric personnel were referring mates to the seminar for treatment for a marital problem. The at times unexpected therapeutic response from this psychotherapeutic modality resulted in such referrals becoming a common experience.

The marital therapist is, above all, a professional who attempts to bring about constructive or creative change in those who come for help. His practice is geared to facilitating therapeutic changes in each mate. Therapeutic change and growth of the person rather than specific maintenance of the marriage is the emphasis and motivating force in this approach. The task is change, whatever the depth of the problem encountered. If no change takes place, the existing problems continue. The change may be from the surface to the deepest levels of psychic functioning. Therapists are change oriented, but the persons presenting their problems may be quite the opposite. They must be taught how to change. The outcome will be the resultant of the forces of (1) the change-oriented therapist and his techniques (with which this book deals), (2) the successful education of the marital partners to a change orientation (therapeutic alliance), (3) the flexibility or inflexibility of the reality pressures, and (4) the most important vector of all—the capacity for creative change within at least one and optimally both of the marriage partners. This last factor includes a flexibility that involves the mates' ability to change their minds, to admit to being wrong, and to learn from experience (Rangell, 1974). Such positive ego attitudes are indicative of the integrity of the ego of the person and contribute to a positive prognosis.

THE PURPOSE AND LIMITATIONS OF TECHNIQUE

This book is about technique—how to bring about change in the field of marital therapy. Since techniques will be stressed, it is important to note that I emphasize techniques while attacking the tendency to overvalue them. My personal experience in using many techniques in treating marriage problems has led me to conclude that there is no magic in any technique. My emphasis is on careful listening to what the patients are saying by a therapist who has sufficient training and intuitiveness to know where the patient is from moment to moment. If the therapist knows what is going on and is creative, he knows what is most likely to bring about change in that person. I believe that therapeutic success does not result from the uniqueness of any one technique but mostly from the elusive capacity for growth, development, learning, and creativity that resides in the person being treated and, to a lesser but very important degree, in the therapist. Studies have shown little significant difference in results from the use of various psychotherapeutic methods. Careful selection of patients using any technique can give excellent statistical results (100%), and as selection becomes less careful, results diminish (Masters and Johnson, 1972). This seems to be a truth encountered repeatedly in medicine, as with new drug therapies or new surgical techniques.

If I advise not to attach magical powers to techniques and to emphasize relatively vague functioning in the patient's ego, such as creativity, capacity for problem solving, learning from experiences, flexibility, and capacity to change, why a book on technique? If techniques are not all important, why not use the same technique for every patient, problem, condition, or diagnosis? Experience does not allow for a recommendation of this simplistic approach. The vital capacity for change (to condense all the ego functions mentioned above into one) can sometimes blossom under any conditions. But this is the exceptional individual and most likely the one who does not come for treatment or who is successful with any therapist and any technique. When large numbers of patients of all types are studied, it becomes clear that some individuals are capable of growth under one set of conditions and not under another. The therapist who is capable of only one approach tries to fit the patients to the approach. Those patients who cannot operate under the therapist's conditions fail to grow. The therapist who can supply a variety of nutrient media, in which a variety of individuals can grow, fits the media to the needs of the patient instead of fitting the patient to the limitations of his capabilities or training.

INDIVIDUALIZATION OF TECHNIQUE

This, then, is a book which stresses first the importance of the patient's capacities in achieving results. Some creative patients with poorly trained therapists utilize less than optimal interpretations and sometimes even incorrect interpretations with good results. Some uncreative patients with the best of therapists have negative therapeutic reactions or no response at all. Like the student who can make his teacher look good, so too a patient can make a therapist look good.

A therapist must know the person with whom he is working, so he can individualize the therapy. Individualization of therapy means utilization of the particular technique most conducive to liberation of the creative forces within that individual. The therapeutic approach used by the therapist avoids repeating those forces which have contributed to the arrest in the development of the individual's capabilities and provides a new opportunity for growth and development within the therapeutic setting. This is the function of technique, and to stress technique in this book is no contradiction to debunking the tendency to impute magical powers to techniques. Techniques are tools in the hands of the craftsman or artist. Limitation of available tools handicaps the most skilled artist, just as a limited variety of colors or inferior pigments would limit even the great painters. Limitation of techniques handicaps the most skilled marital therapist and his patients, as does the lack of creativity to invent new techniques crafted specifically for the individual who is presenting his problems.

In keeping with the emphasis on the patient's capacities in achieving results, I wish to refer to the work of H. V. Dicks. He distinguishes marital therapy from psychotherapy of individuals by his emphasis on the marital therapist's responsibility to help maintain the marital relationship. He introduces a primarily "social, public weal focus" into his definition of marital therapy (Dicks, 1967) and contrasts this with Kubie's emphasis that the individual's mental health comes first. The difficulty with such statements is that they leave the impression that the therapist and his approach are the determining factors in the outcome of therapy. My experiences and those of other therapists with whom I have worked dictate a different emphasis: the outcome is determined by the forces within the marital partners and not by the biases of the therapist. The therapist is the hand servant of the forces within the patient and not the determining force in the outcome of therapy. As stated by Wheelis: "In the process of personality change the role of the psychiatrist is catalytic. As a cause he is sometimes necessary, never sufficient" (Wheelis, 1973).

In summary, the creative patient can make any therapist or any technique, no matter how wild either may be, look good. At the other extreme is the type of patient who goes from therapist to therapist, from technique to technique, and makes them all look bad. In between is a large group of patients with whom the matching of patient with therapist and most helpful technique can determine success or failure, for the benefit of or detriment to the patient. A note of warning is required to differentiate the creative patient described above and the pseudo-creative type. They may look alike at first to the inexperienced observer or when judged over too short a period of time by therapists with high therapeutic ambitions. An example was a young clergyman who was fervent in his religion until he came in contact with pastoral counseling. He then enthusiastically embraced psychoanalysis and became a fervent lay therapist. He then abandoned this activity to move to California and become fervently devoted to the drug culture. The creative type of patient to which I refer is judged from a perspective of thirty years and not from a vantage point of a few months or a few years; only the latter view leads one to attribute superior effectiveness to any new therapy.

Who Should Have Marital Therapy?

Who should have marital therapy and who should not? An obvious response is: those coming with the presenting problem as a marital problem should have marital therapy; those who don't should not. The next response could be that those in dyadic or family therapy who in the course of therapy present a serious marital problem should have marital therapy. However, this is too simplistic a reply and not in keeping with the position developed in the preceding paragraphs.

Clinical experience has shown that we do not as yet accurately know in all instances, by preliminary interviews or psychological testing, who will be successful in such therapy as psychoanalysis or intensive psychotherapy. Sometimes, despite careful screening, serious mistakes are made. All preliminary judgments are tentative and need frequent reevaluation to determine more accurately what a particular patient really wants or really can utilize. The therapist who is capable of such reevaluations as treatment progresses can answer the question more accurately. Those initially deemed in need of marital therapy may turn out to need individual therapy, or vice-versa.

An obvious example of initial misrepresentation is the couple who, although they present themselves for marital therapy, soon reveal that either the husband or wife really wants therapy to help get a divorce and to have the other mate accept it. Another example is the individual in dyadic therapy for symptoms such as phobias or depression who discovers there is a marital problem that has to be resolved before the symptoms will recede.

Not only do we not know in all instances by preliminary interviews or psychological testing who should or should not have marital therapy, we also cannot easily determine which types of marital therapy would be best. It requires constant listening and frequent reevaluation to answer these questions for any one marital couple. Although these conclusions may be humbling to therapists, they form a solid foundation for therapeutic activities and use of techniques.

REFERENCES

Cookerly, J. R. (1973), The outcome of the six major forms of marriage counseling compared: a pilot study. *Journal of Marriage and the Family*, 35, 4: 608-611.

Dicks, H. V. (1967), *Marital Tensions*. New York: Basic Books, pp. 229-231.

Framo, J. L. (1975), Personal reflections of a family therapist. *Journal of Marriage and Family Counseling*, 1, 1: 22.

Freud, A. (1960), Introduction. In *The Psychoanalytic Study of the Child*, 15: 378. New York: International Universities Press.

Freud, S. (1909), Analysis of a phobia in a five-year-old boy. *Standard Edition*, 10: 3-149. London: Hogarth Press, 1955.

Martin, P. A., and Lief, H. I. (1973), Resistance to innovation in psychiatric training as exemplified by marital therapy. In *Psychiatry: Education and Image*, ed. G. Usdin. New York: Brunner/Mazel, pp. 151-165.

Masters, W. H., and Johnson, V. E. (1972), The rapid treatment of human sexual dysfunction. In *Progress in Group and Family Therapy*, eds. C. J. Sager and H. S. Kaplan. New York: Brunner/Mazel, pp. 553-563.

Rangell, L. (1974), A psychoanalytic perspective. *International J. Psychoanal.*, 55: 3-12.

Sager, C. J., Grundlach, R., Kremer, M., Lenz, R., and Royce, J. R. (1968), The married in treatment. *Archives of General Psychiatry*, 19: 206.

Stone, I. (1971), *The Passions of the Mind*. New York: Doubleday and Co., Inc., p. 778.

Wheelis, A. (1973), *How People Change*. New York: Harper and Row, p. 7.

2

Psychological Patterns and Normal Values in Marriage

BY DELINEATING TYPES OF psychopathological marriages we can derive normal values for marriage, which in turn allow for highlighting those changes required to establish a healthy marriage pattern. My conceptualization is in contrast to Haley's statement (Haley, 1963) that there is no formal description of pathological marriages and therefore no theory of what changes must be brought about. The four patterns described below are those most commonly encountered in treating marriage problems.

The unconscious reasons for a particular marriage pattern determine the type of problem that will arise in the relationship. This makes possible the classification of pathological relations which follows. Of course these categories are not rigidly held or clearly demarcated entities into which one can fit all pathological marriages. Some types overlap, and there are elements of one kind in another. Yet by categorizing psychopathological conditions, we are able to conduct such useful research as comparing outcome studies of similar entities between different groups of therapists or different techniques of therapy.

FOUR PATHOLOGICAL MARRIAGE PATTERNS

It is medical tradition to derive normal values of body functions from prior investigation of abnormal functioning. When an organ of

15

the body is functioning smoothly, there is often little incentive to study its mechanisms. When it gets out of order, our attention is called to those mechanisms responsible for its failure to function. It becomes easier to understand how the unit functions normally after understanding its pathology. Similarly, Freud pointed out that the study of psychopathology has been of enormous service in contributing to our knowledge of the "normal" psychology of everyday life. Psychoanalysis has already made considerable progress in formulating scientific generalizations by making use of highlights that psychopathology can throw upon the dynamic mechanisms of normal behavior. Likewise, in working with patients who were extremely unhappy in their marriages, my attention was called to those mechanisms responsible for the failure of the marriage to function well. The four marriage patterns I shall describe here illustrate various types of psychopathology and allow for the derivation of "normal" values for a healthy, smoothly functioning marriage.

1. The Love "Sick" Wife and the "Cold Sick" Husband
(Martin and Bird, 1959)

This pattern—the "hysterical" wife and "obsessional" husband—is the most common and most difficult psychotherapeutic problem we have encountered. The first such patients we studied were upper middle class couples seen in the private practice of psychiatry. We first emphasized that the husbands' ability to afford simultaneous psychotherapy for themselves and their wives was an important illustration of the men's adequate talents and sufficient ego strengths. It is this strength of the ego that characterizes the husbands and which markedly contrasts with the weakness of the wives' ego. Further studies, however, encompassing some 200 couples over a period of twenty-five years, showed that this pattern occurs at all socioeconomic levels and is also determined by unconscious factors involved in the choice of mates.

The Wives. This clinical entity is determined by the picture presented by the wives. No one wife illustrated all of the features to be enumerated, but when the individual variations of the theme were removed, they proved to be remarkably similar. The wife comes for treatment first because she has been experiencing severe anxiety, depressions, or incapacitating physical symptoms. She is no longer able to manage the home, care for the children, or meet her social obligations. She may have been taking tranquilizers for years under the guidance of her family physician. She is emotionally decompensated and bordering on an even more severe regression. From the first interview with the psychiatrist, or as soon as the depression lifts in a depressed patient, she claims that her sickness is due entirely to the coldness and cruelty of her husband. She insists that he does not care about what she wants or what she feels. She states emphatically that she has a deep capacity to love, but that her husband is cold, unsympathetic, cruel, or psychotic.

She gives countless examples to prove how emotionally inadequate he is by showing how he didn't do what she felt he should have done. This, to her, is evidence of his inability to love. Despite her symptoms, she denies her intrapsychic conflicts by stressing the interpersonal relationship in the marriage. She complains that her husband is either sexually inadequate or oversexed. She blames her sexual unresponsiveness on her husband. A stalemate in her treatment leads to the wife's statement that her husband must go into treatment too or she will not get well, or a divorce will be necessary. To her, the only solution is a change in her husband. Her opinion, forcibly expressed, is that the husband, even though symptom free, is sicker than she is. Sometimes it is the inexperienced psychiatrist himself who makes this statement, or the desperate psychiatrist who cannot reach the wife and who must accept her conditions and hope to effect some change in her through the husband.

These wives are often difficult to diagnose. They may be considered hysterical personalities or be placed in the broad diagnostic category of borderline characters. Their relation to their husband is of a symbiotic, parasitic type. They suffer from the narcissistic problem of low self-esteem. They do not experience a fixed, firm, stable personality of their own as distinct from the need-satisfying objects. Being outer directed in the presence of others, they look for approval and help to establish who they are and how worthwhile they are.

The picture of these women is so characteristic that they are easy to recognize within a few minutes in the first interview, and it is easy to predict just what they are going to say for the rest of the hour. They can be recognized in any age group before or after marriage. I remember a seventy-year old woman who came because of a depression. She had been married fifty years, had children, grandchildren, and great-grandchildren. I asked her what was troubling her. Her tale of woe was typical. Her husband did not love her. He paid attention to other women, kidding and joking with waitresses when they went to restaurants. Never had there been any infidelity.

High school girls come, tearful and depressed, because boyfriends do not pay enough attention to them. Little girls are often reared differently from boys. For example, they are received in a different way when they reach out for approval from adults. Girls who have a strong need for approval usually find it. It is acceptable behavior. But boys who need approval may be scorned badly. Such experiences ill prepare girls for the pubertal, adolescent, and adult one-to-one relations with men, wherein their belief is that it is the responsibility of their husbands to relieve all their anxieties, desires, and unfulfilled needs. Such an attitude may only serve to arouse whatever dormant passive-resistant traits the men may have. They may treat the wives with scorn as they themselves were treated as children when they demanded love.

To the male therapist these wives are tender traps. They are often vocal, emotional, enthusiastic, artistic, talented, and attractive. They seem to make quick, strong, positive transferences to the therapist; they seem to believe so greatly in the value of treatment that they declare everyone should be in treatment, especially their husbands. They are hysterical personalities whose structures may be considered to be on a genital level but who really are deeply-rooted oral characters, quick to agree in order to win favor but unable to hold a position verbally agreed upon. The following is a detailed picture of one of these wives.

Mrs. A. entered psychiatric treatment because she was suffering from severe attacks of anxiety that caused her physical incapacitation. In her opening hours, accompanied by crying and shaking, she expressed fears of her husband becoming deathly sick. This abnormal concern for her husband proved to be a projection of her hostility against him, for it was followed by a period of innumerable complaints against him. She claimed that he was cold, unloving, and did not want to do what she wanted him to do. She blamed all her symptoms on him. She blamed him for all of her troubles. She blamed all her problems on his not loving her as she wanted to be loved. She complained that he forced her to take all the responsibilities for their children. She attempted to show that he was inadequate.

As the hours produced more material, it became obvious that it was she who lived a dependent, parasitic life, with her husband as the host. She would not walk on her own two feet and go in the direction she wanted to go. She rode on her husband's back and complained when he did not go in the direction she wanted him to go. If she tried to do anything on her own, she developed severe symptoms of diarrhea, frequency of urination, nausea or vomiting. After the birth of each of her children, she had to force herself out of bed in order to take care of them. Her first child was sent to summer camp when only three years old. Throughout the many years that followed, whenever it was time to visit her children at camp, instead of being eager to see them she would become nauseated to the degree of becoming incapacitated. She was cold, critical, and hostile to her children and continually called her oldest daughter by her own hated sister's name. In short, she had no identification as a loving mother of her children.

Her analysis uncovered tremendous hatred against her own mother who, because of an inadequate husband, had "worked like a dog all her life." Her mother's assumption of both parental roles left no time for love or attention to Mrs. A. Her mother would develop rage reactions against her husband and children when she became physically and emotional exhausted. Mrs. A.'s reaction of hatred caused her to swear to herself during her childhood never to be like her mother. This serious struggle with her mother resulted in resistance to emotional growth and development; she became fixated in an inadequate, parasitic baby position in relation to her mother; as such she could constantly complain that her mother did not love her. This parasitic relation to her mother was retained until she was married, when it was automatically transferred to her husband.

When this patient, unsuccessful in her home, entered into club activities and community charitable work, she became panicky and quit. She rationalized her inadequacy by saying she did not like the kind of women who did this work. When she went out as a guest to a country club, she became panicky and ran home. As usual she denied her inadequacy and claimed that the women who played golf and bridge were silly and superficial. The same thing happened when she joined an organization devoted to doing charity work in the community. These women could hardly be criticized, but she did it. During treatment she attempted to gain her independence by going to college to become a teacher. But she could not concentrate on her reading. She stated it was silly to work so hard, became panicky, and quit. She joined a little symphony group which required only attendance and financial support. Since her husband was not interested, she dropped out. This turned out to be her pattern. So it went, up and down the line. She deprecated and destroyed every resource available to people for sublimation of drives and establishment of a solid identity.

Mrs. A. had no clear sense of identity. She had a series of quick "as-if" identifications with various characteristics, but she did not know who or what she was as an adult. Her unconscious identification was with a puking, diaper-soaked, abandoned baby. From the material presented above, it was possible to place her in the broad diagnostic category of borderline patients who suffer from the specific narcissistic problem of management of their self-esteem. When there is a real or fantasied slight or disapproval from the other person, such patients react with a near psychotic rage which wipes out any shred of existing self-identity. These women may thus be considered to be love addicts or people addicts. Identification with the object exceeds in importance object relationships.

The Husbands. The clinical picture of the husbands which completes this marital pattern contrasts markedly. The husbands were intelligent, educated men who held positions of responsibility. They were at least competent and some were even brilliant in their fields. They were respected in their work and in their communities. They were not emotionally decompensated and not given to drugs or alcohol. They differed radically from their wives in not showing much emotion. They were more intellectual, logical, and reasonable in their relationships to other people and problems. They were adequate to the requirements of life outside of the home, but varied in their adequacy within the home in reaction to the wives' unrelenting involvements with them.

The greatest variation among the husbands lay in their own evaluation of a need for psychotherapy. At one extreme there were those who were adamant in the view that they needed no help and that the problem was entirely the wife's. Some of these would not even come for an evaluation. The middle group were willing to do anything to alleviate the disturbed marital conditions and were eager for help for themselves. At the other extreme were some who were beginning to doubt their own senses and to think that perhaps their wives were right about the problems being entirely the fault of the husbands.

When in treatment, the picture presented by these men differed markedly from their wives' presentations. It was the picture of apparently well-adjusted men who had been successful in their occupational activities, in their social relationships, and in operating under pressure. This suggested that they were of sufficient emotional maturity to warrant being included in the broad classification of the so-called "normal" adult. Despite this classification, their treatment revealed that beneath the surface of their characteristic attitudes and defenses was a ferocity of emotional conflicts. There were great restrictions and ever impoverishment of instinctual expression and in some a prominence of primitive ego defenses. In some, the ferocity of the conflicts was as great as that of their wives. Why then were the wives sick and these men considered relatively healthy? The vital difference lay in their egos.

While it may be true that normality might be considered to be a fiction or a fantasy, a person can be considered ego-strong who, while defending himself against the inner drives, has not deprived himself of energy for the sustaining of ego functions in consonance with instinctual needs. When these men were judged by such a yardstick, their treatment revealed marked differences as to the degree of their ego strength. Some were unable to show feelings of closeness, intimacy, anger, or love. Their superegos and reality egos triumphed at the expense of a restriction of libido. That is why they were not felt to be warm people. They suffered from the problem of intimacy in close relationships. They had fixed, rigid character structures with a sense of personal continuity and systematization that was in marked contrast to their wives. Some were considered "so-called normal," others had obsessive-compulsive character structures, and a third type tended toward being paranoid.

In contrast to the wives, these are patients whom psychotherapists frequently do not like. They either refuse to come for treatment or in treatment show little need or respect for help. They are often stand-offish, suspicious, and, compared to the wives' rapid involvements, have a paranoid approach that may antagonize the inexperienced therapist.

The Marriage Pattern. These are marriages in which a reversal takes place after the marriage ceremony. At the onset of the marriage, the wife seems to have the upper hand. She is pretty or vivacious and the husband is plain, shy, or subdued. She appears to be exciting and entertaining or promises a knowledge of the arts, music, and the humanities which the husband lacks. During the years that follow, the husband continues to grow in character, becomes successful in business or his profession, becomes more adequate in dealing with people, loses his shyness, and gains confidence in himself. He is a worker. The wife, in contrast, is a talker. Despite her protests, she does not feel motherly, does not enjoy responsibilities in the home, and is incapable of establishing herself outside of the home as she flits from one opportunity to another. The difficulty in the relationship is that the partners, unable to develop and integrate viable patterns of intimacy, introduce into the marriage distortions and limitations of experience which restrict or even bar intimacy (Barnett, 1971).

This contrast between mates is strikingly noticeable in societies such as Washington, D.C., where there is a concentration of very successful men and the wives they married when they were young. One longtime observer, a journalist, wrote a column stating that Washington, D.C. after dark is the most depressing city he had seen. At cocktail parties one meets couples whose presence there is determined by the success of the husbands, who have become leaders in their fields. The depressing picture was that of their wives. Even if the marriages had started with the mates as equals, the wives had not grown through the years and the contrast to their husbands was appalling to the writer. It is appalling to the wives too. Their narcissistic needs are depleted and they suffer devastating blows to their self-esteem, leading to varying defense mechanisms with symptoms of phobias, depression, or projections onto the husbands of the unacceptable portions of their own personalities.

The study of the wives' personalities and our conclusions in our early studies and in follow-up studies after thirty years show an amazing consistency—a sameness with minor changes except for the few whose therapies were successful. Irreparable defects in ego functioning often perpetuated a tendency to regression under stress and prevented completion of maturation. In contrast, the pictures of some of the husbands after these years had changed remarkably. Some continued to grow and develop through the years in their careers. Only one small group (20 percent), who recognized no need for help, found that the methods which had brought them success early in life proved to be too rigid and inflexible. When need for change at work took place, they kept their same approach. They had been promoted above the level of their capacities. This, together with their relative inability to understand people's feelings, caused them difficulties at the higher level of functioning. The early paranoid attitudes became intensified. With later-life failures, not uncommon in business, they became emotionally decompensated; some developed paranoid psychoses. Interestingly enough, for this group the truth in the accusations hurled at them by their wives early in marriage, which was not clearly discernible by psychiatric evaluation, became clear. Within the wives' paranoid projections were kernels of truth. An individual may function well in many areas with no marked recognition of a problem with intimacy that is exposed early in the intensity of the marriage relationship. When later changes occurred, these marriages slipped into the paranoid type described later in this chapter.

2. An "In-Search-of-a-Mother" Marriage (Martin and Bird, 1962)

In this specific entity, the "hysterical" husband with an "obsessional" wife, the husband seeks out a therapist because a crisis has arisen in his marriage. He is having an affair with another woman and plans to marry her. External circumstances have blocked his plans and precipitate his breakdown. When he comes to the marital therapist on his own, it is mainly to find out how to get what he wants so desperately—the other woman—without making his wife vindictive. Some of these men do not come willingly. They have been rejected by the other woman and want to return to their family, but they are forced to seek help by their angry wives who now refuse to take them back without psychotherapy.

The picture of the men involved with this type of problem broke down into two groups. The smaller percentage (20 percent) fell into the active or mastering group, which will be described here but will not be used to derive normal values. It was made up of individuals with a history of being successful in whatever they did. They were opportunists whose relationships were shallow, allowing them to move from one situation to a more advantageous one. They could not conceive of defeat in their wishes to marry their mistresses. Those who came on their own wished to borrow from the psychotherapist the fantasied know-how of getting what one wants. They could not stand feelings of helplessness and only broke down or became depressed when it became evident they would not get what they wanted. They had sociopathic traits in their characters.

The passive, dependent group searched for mothering not to master but to be taken care of. This was a manifestation of their regressive, demanding positions and acceptance of positions of helplessness. They were in search of loving and protection. They did not manage their personal affairs well, competed poorly with other men, and turned to women for consolation and support. They bordered on irresponsibility and impulsivity. Alcoholism was a common symptom in this group. They were oral characters with hysterical personalities.

Eighty percent of this clinical entity were of the passive type. The pattern then would best be described as one of a passive-dependent husband and a dominant wife. The husband panics when he is in situations of independence and turns to a strong woman as a child turns to a mother when under stress.

The Wives. These wives were characteristically excellent mothers in terms of consistency, reliability, and dependability. They all stated that they loved their husbands, and they showed a capacity to endure traumatic marital experiences. They were more like the husbands in the preceding pattern—obsessive-compulsive personalities. Divorces were rare as they usually accepted the return of their husbands. They noted that changes in the marriage relationship occurred when the children came and they were no longer able to devote themselves exclusively to the husbands. The husbands had then looked elsewhere for exclusive devotion. Closer observation of these wives exposed a need to organize, dominate, and control others. Though they did help others, they tended to dominate them.

The "Other Women." These women were capable, competent individuals much like the wives. If married, they were capable mothers and wives in their own right. Their involvement with these men seemed based on their response to a needy person. Also, marriage to these men often would have meant marked social and economic improvement. In addition, the men tended to be excellent lovers with great capacity for physical intimacy. As lovers the "other women" appeared to be more responsive to sensuousness and love than the wives, but the impression was that after marriage they would be like the wives.

When final decisions were to be made, however, these women were more realistic than the men, and if married often refused to divorce their husbands. Their children were more important to them than their lovers. If unmarried or widowed, they were willing to marry if their lovers could get a divorce. When this happened, we had a different clinical picture. Instead of the in-search-of-a-mother husband being the first to come for treatment, it was the wife who came to find out how to recapture her husband from the "other woman."

The Marriage Pattern. The pattern is not uncommon. The man marries young, even before he has finished his education or is able to earn a living. He appears to marry for love. His wife works and helps him in his career until the children come. Simultaneous with her inability, due to circumstances, to take complete care of him, he becomes financially self-sufficient and looks for another woman who will be free to take care of him and who may be younger, prettier and apparently more sensuous.

3. The *"Double-Parasite"* Marriage (Hysterical-Hysterical or Dependent-Dependent)

These marriages are made up of two people who cannot swim, clutching each other desperately and drowning together. They are a combination of a passive-dependent husband married to a passive-dependent wife. The couples we saw in clinical practice came from two socioeconomic extremes. Some were seen in a free outpatient psychiatry department of a general hospital. They were indigents. Neither partner was able to carry the load of the marriage. Alcoholism, drugs, anxiety, depression and inability to work characterized these couples.

The other couples of this type were seen in private practice and were very wealthy. However, the wealth had been inherited either by one or both mates. They were emotionally incapable of being good parents and were hostilely projecting their inadequacies onto the mate. They were filled with anxieties and neurotic symptoms as defenses. The two living together did not quite make one ego. They formed a parasitic due of two cactuses who could not live together and also could not live alone. Each expected to be taken care of by the other and when expectations were not met responded with primitive rage reactions or panic reactions often accompanied by phobic formations.

The marriage pattern involved each mate expecting the other one to take the responsibility for making the marriage work and neither one being capable of growth or of fulfilling the other's needs. Compared to the first two marriage patterns, the difficulty in this type emerges more quickly after the marriage ceremony, with phobic symptoms in one or both sometimes emerging before children arrive and sometimes during the honeymoon period. The couples who inherited wealth were additionally handicapped by family expectations based on their education and social position.

4. The Paranoid Marriage

Of the four types of clinically disturbed marriages being used here for the derivation of normal values for marriage, the paranoid type is most helpful in highlighting the need for separation and individuation of each mate. There are several patterns within the scope of the paranoid marriages. At one end of the spectrum is the pathological condition called *folie à deux*, in which the marital pair get along well together by sharing the same delusions but come into conflict with reality. At the other extreme is "conjugal paranoia," whereby one partner's delusional system is focused on the behavior of the mate, thus allowing the patient to function without conflict in non-marital life situations but horribly in the marriage. In between are various degrees of the mates holding in common a number of ideas, values, prejudices, distortions or denials of reality, which makes the marriage harmonious; or of disagreement over conflicting ideas, values, prejudices, distortions, or denials of reality of either mate, which makes the marriage argumentative.

Folie à deux. This condition was first reported in 1860, when two members of the same family were hospitalized on the same day suffering from similar delusions (Cameron, 1959). This is a psychosis of association, with the transference of delusional ideas or abnormal behavior from one individual to others with whom some intimate relationship exists. Typically, a dominant, psychotic person provokes a delusional development in a relatively dependent, submissive mate. The dependent one usually recovers after a few months of separation. Paranoid reactions and paranoid schizophrenia with persecutory delusions are the usual psychotic pictures. This occurs in persons who have been living together in intimate contact for a long time (Gralnick, 1942). Experience with this type of couple indicates that the dependent person faces the choice of fighting the delusional system of the mate and chancing the permanent loss of that mate or accepting the delusional system in order to maintain the relationship. H. Deutsch interprets delusion formation in the dependent person as an attempt to recover a lost object through identification with its delusional system (Deutsch, 1938). A recent study concludes that such defects as schizophrenia, mental subnormality, dementia, and certain personality disorders may predispose the individual to acquire the delusion of his partner. The social milieu, a precipitant in some cases, will determine content of the delusional system (Soni and Rockley, 1974).

The Paranoid Marriage. Less bizarre and more frequent than *folie à deux* is the paranoid marriage. The paranoid marriage transforms reality through illusionary notions (Richter, 1974). The mates overvalue certain protective ideas or ideologies, behind which they mobilize and defend themselves and change the world through active, systematic reinterpretations.

This is a sick marriage in which the two partners are intertwined, wrapped around each other in a suicide-of-the-individuated-self pact against the world. They are in harmony with each other because they share delusions and illusions and build a fence around the family unit. They create the illusion of getting along well together by externalizing their internal group problem and seeking in the world around them targets for reproaches that are really aimed at each other and originally, mostly unconsciously, against their own egos. The active, dominant member of the family demands a friend-or-foe way of thinking. This couple does not come for therapy. They are seen when the bizarre ideas get the dominant member into difficulty with authorities at work. If the wife is the paranoid individual she tends to remain isolated in the home. She is unable to hold a job. She gets into arguments with friends, neighbors, relatives, and the children's teachers. Only at home *when her word is not questioned* can she get along with others. If the husband is the paranoid individual, he has serious quarrels with his supervisors at work. To work for another male amounts to emasculation or, on an unconscious level, annihilation (Jacobs, 1974).

When the above picture begins to deteriorate and the couple comes for therapy, the most common picture seen in the paranoid pattern is the dominant mate's mobilization of constant, uncompromising enmity toward the other mate who is no longer accepting the paranoid ideation and is fighting for survival of the self. It is the latter, struggling to survive, who comes for help. This struggle for survival is usually easier for therapists to understand than the choice of comradeship-in-arms (when overawed members of the family become slavish followers), until the therapist experiences the terrifying violence and determination of the active mate, who becomes enraged whenever his or her authority is questioned. This rage reveals a desperate struggle for survival as an individual. The dynamic factor that explains the slavish submission is the helplessness and inability to separate and to take care of oneself that is present in the dependent mate and children. It is this inability to separate which forces the raping of their senses for the sake of protection and care. To maintain separate thinking capacities, the dependent mate needs both a firmly established personal identity and the ability to stand alone. In contrast, the acceptance of the paranoid system of thought promises instantaneous discharge of all threatening interpersonal tension.

The active contribution to the marriage pattern by the so-called passive partner is an important recognition reported in the literature (Dupont and Grunebaum, 1968). They report a study of nine married women with the diagnosis of paranoid state. The wives were characterized by definite paranoid delusions without hallucinations and by preservation of the personality and intelligence despite the psychosis. These women had chosen husbands who were passive, socially isolated and unable to directly express anger or sexual feelings. The men were willing victims and active participants in the bizarre behavior of their wives. By cooperating with their wives, they contributed to the worsening of the illness. If confinement to a hospital became necessary, it came about not as a decision of the husbands, nor even with their consent, but through intervention from the outside. The "passive" mate cannot stand the separation from the "active" partner. No matter how disturbed the psychotic partner becomes, staying together is experienced as more reassuring than the experience of loss, separation, and loneliness. The passive partner's behavior is both positively adaptive to the mate's psychiatric disturbance and yet an active participant in fostering the mate's psychosis, though this might appear contradictory at first glance. The marital system meets important psychological needs of both the husband and wife.

Conjugal Paranoia. The clinical entity in which the paranoid delusions and pathological attitudes have been directed against the mate has been called "conjugal paranoia" (Revitch, 1954). The pathological attitudes of the active mate, characterized by fault-finding, humiliating, degrading, demoralizing, and destructive acts against the other mate, may precede by many years the outbreak of frank paranoid delusions. Conjugal relations (everything having to do with responsibilities as a mate) induce in the patient a general feeling of inadequacy with which he copes by utilizing the defense mechanisms of projection, reaction formation, delusions, and even hallucinations. Early in the marriage the difficult mate may be considered just "jealous" or "mean." The delusional system which appears later often involves pathological jealousy and accusations of infidelity. There is a litigious type of conjugal paranoiac who initiates court action against the mate, complaining of nonsupport, infidelity or abuse. Because the delusions are so well systematized and may have some factual basis, and since the patient is mentally lucid, the lawyer, judge, immediate family, and family physician may be won over by the paranoid mate. Careful investigation and close scrutiny, however, will disclose the distortions and exaggerations in the accusations, as well as the precipitating activities of the "aggrieved" mate which cause the reactions in the other that form the factual basis for the complaints.

When the husband is the paranoid mate, the passive wife tends to be prone to depressions. The husband is overly concerned with his masculinity, resulting in jealousy and suspiciousness. He denies intimacy with his wife and dreads the danger (to him) of loss of his self.

The "Normal" Marriage Values Derived from Psychopathological Patterns

The outstanding pathological factor in the "Love-Sick" Wife and "Cold-Sick" Husband marriage pattern was the wife's inability to support herself. She could not stand being alone and thus could not stand on her own. In an unprotected situation her cognitive functions became overwhelmed with emotions. She then became illogical and irrational, necessitating the taking over of these functions by her mate. The "Cold-Sick" Husband's outstanding psychological problem was that he could not stand intimacy. The wife's overwhelming need for intimacy causes him to withdraw further behind his defenses. He could support himself but could not emotionally support others. He could be alone and separate but not together and intimate. The marriage therefore did not involve a constantly functioning, working relationship, supportive for each mate and protective of the children in the family.

In the "In-Search-of-a-Mother" marriage pattern, the passive type husband was the one incapable of being self-supporting, separate, and of maintaining cognitive functioning without another person's help. If it were not given to him upon demand, he decompensated or found another woman to support him. The wives and the other women in this pattern were uniformly capable and adequate in their own right as well as being able to care for others. To the extent that their capabilities were not determined by a need to care for dependent-clinging beings, they were healthy. The more they were enslaved and driven by such a need which they were unable to master, the more they deviated from the norm.

The Double Parasite pattern involved an inability of both mates to support themselves and others, with no formation of the supportive structure which distinguishes a relationship capable of forming a stable marriage.

The *Folie à Deux* type of paranoid marriage illustrated no structure separating and yet uniting two individuals. It illustrated a fusion with no spaces in the togetherness. The dominant mate forged a bond of enslavement around the submissive mate so neither could be alone or react individually to the stimuli from reality.

From the above characteristics of psychopathology come the following conclusions about the healthy marriage.

In the studies which accompanied Action For Mental Health several years ago, one section dealt with the definition of mental health. It proved difficult or impossible to define without many qualifying statements. But the minimal definition of mental health in the American culture was the ability to stand on one's own two feet without too much imposition upon others. In addition a marriage creates a need to be capable of supporting others. This mutual supportiveness creates the unifying framework which neither individual can form alone. A healthy marriage, then, is a union between two individuals who are self-supporting and supportive-of-others and who are committed to their marriage union. These "normal" values for marriage, which are derived from psychopathological marriages, are in keeping with psychoanalytic concepts of psychosocial development from the early, symbiotic mother-child relationship through separation and individuation to maturity, wisdom, knowledge and the capacity to feel kinship with and love for human beings other than oneself. Ideally in marriage, independence is equal, dependence mutual, and obligation reciprocal, but there are many variations from this ideal which still allow for a "normal" marriage.

Normal values here as in other areas of human functioning allow for wide ranges before becoming pathological. Marriage of course is not a static state but is one phase of the individual's life cycle. It is one wherein further growth and development can occur through the intimate experience with the mate. Marriage is a state in which mates can help one another to reach the full status of being responsible, autonomous, separate individuals—or else, in the intensity and intimacy of the relationship, cause serious regression and psychopathology. Marriage has the capacity for growth or destructiveness.

The "normal" marriage, then, involves a relationship between two equally self-supporting and supportive adults. Obviously, in nature this ideal is never present 100 percent. It is a reference point that helps to explain both adequate functioning and malfunctioning. No person remains the same in each stage of his life cycle. And although all people are created equal, there are vast individual differences in capability, strength, capacity for understanding. In general, a mutual commitment to each other forms a structure in marriage that is protective, supportive, and conducive to growth and change for both partners and for their children.

ON DERIVING VALUES FROM PATHOLOGICAL VERSUS HEALTHY MARRIAGES

The preceding method of deriving normal from pathological is subject to the cautions found in the literature about the danger of applying insights learned primarily from pathological relationships to developing relationships. It is recognized that what is needed is research on "enriched" couples from various social strata to discover more about the ingredients of enriched marriages (Miller, et al., 1975).

With this in mind, from the beginning of our research into marital problems we have concomitantly studied all available sources of "enriched" marriages to double-check our conclusions. Studies of normal, healthy marriages give the conclusions drawn here an even sharper and more vivid focus.

A recent development in American studies of marriage gives promise of further insights into healthy marriages. This is the development of marriage and family enrichment programs in North America. This is a movement for couples who have what they perceive to be a fairly well-functioning marriage and who wish to make their marriage even more mutually satisfying (Otto, 1975). Its aim is to stress the improvement of the relationship by the development of its un-appropriated inner resources, with goals of "marital growth," "marital potential," and "marital health." Rather than being remedial, it is a preventive concept of facilitating positive growth (Mace, and Mace, 1975). These are the same emphases derived from working with pathological marriages where evidence is overwhelming as to the resistance to growth and development and the rigid maintenance of stultifying conditions. Studies of normal marriages confirm the conclusions drawn from psychopathologic patterns.

REFERENCES

Barnett, J. (1971), Narcissism and dependency in the obsessional-hysteric marriage. *Family Process*, 10: 75-83.

Cameron, N. (1959), Paranoid conditions and paranoia. In *American Handbook of Psychiatry*, Vol. I, ed. S. Arieti. New York: Basic Books, p. 527.

Deutsch, H. (1938), *Folie à deux. Psychoanal. Quart.*, 7: 307.

Dupont, R. L., and Grunebaum, H. (1968), Willing victims: the husbands of paranoid women. *Amer. J. Psychiat.*, 125: 47-55.

Gralnick, A. (1942), *Folie à deux*, "the psychoses of association." *Psychiatric Quarterly*, 16: 230.

Haley, J. (1963), Marriage therapy. *Archives of General Psychiatry*, 8: 213-234.

Jacobs, L. I. (1974), Sexual problems and personalities in four types of marriage. *Medical Aspects of Human Sexuality*, 8: 160-181.

Mace, D. R., and Mace, V. C. (1975), Marriage enrichment—wave of the future? *The Family Coordinator*, 24, 2: 131-135.

Martin, P. A., and Bird, H. W. (1959), The "love-sick" wife and the "cold-sick" husband. *Psychiatry*, 22: 246.

Martin, P. A., and Bird, H. W. (1962), One type of the "in-search-of-a-mother" marital pattern. *Psychiat. Quart.*, 36: 283-293.

Miller, S., Corrales, R., and Wackman, D. B. (1975), Recent progress in understanding and facilitating marital communication. *The Family Coordinator*, 24, 2: 143-156.

Otto, H. A. (1975), Marriage and family enrichment programs in North America—report and analysis. *The Family Coordinator*, 24, 2: 137-142.

Revitch, E. (1954), The problem of conjugal paranoia. *Diseases of the Nervous System*, pp. 271-277.

Richter, H. E. (1974), *The Family as Patient*. New York: Farrar, Straus, Giroux.

Soni, S. D., and Rockley, G. J. (1974), Socio-clinical substrates of *folie à deux*. *Brit. J. Psychiat.*, 125: 230-235.

3

Sexual Aspects of Marriage: Normal Values Derived from Psychopathology

INTRODUCTION

THE PRECEDING CHAPTER developed "normal" values for marriage with major emphasis on the personality structures, the interpersonal relations, and the marital pattern of the mates. I wish now to include a picture of the sexual psychopathology encountered in treating marital problems, in order to derive normal values for this area. My experience has indicated that sexual problems in marriage can best be understood and then treated in marital therapy by the recognition of the following three dominant areas and their varying influences and combinations: 1) Intercourse per se without physical or emotional intimacy, for which the term *lust* is usually used in the literature. This involves a physical discharge of libidinal drive. (1) Physical intimacy, for which the term *sensuousness* is usually used. This involves the sensuous pleasures, such as touching, kissing, stroking, petting, embracing and oral sensual activities, pre- and post-intercourse. There has been a tremendous increase in emphasis on sensuousness in the mass media and by experts in sexuality. Sensitivity training groups flourish throughout America, stressing aspects of intimacy and particularly freedom to experience pleasures in physical intimacies. (3) Emotional intimacy, usually referred to as

34

love. This involves the interpersonal relationship (talking, admiration, adoration, internal excitement, warmth, yearning, missing the other person).

Variations on Three Sexual Themes Encountered in Treatment of Marriage Problems as Presented by Patients

1. *Lust*

Sex—intercourse per se, without physical intimacy (sensuousness) or emotional intimacy (love).

Wife. "My husband is like a truck driver. He comes home, we have intercourse. No talking, no lovemaking. No preparation, no love. He is an animal. All he wants is intercourse. I can't stand it. I want him to talk to me, to caress me, to kiss me. I love kissing. ("Love-sick" wife, who needs physical and emotional intimacy for survival.)

Husband. "My wife says that she cannot stand me anymore. She wants no intimacy. When I demand it, she will have intercourse. No preliminary, no foreplay, no talking. She lets me have intercourse with her and that is it. No response on her part. But she does her duty. I can't stand it." (Passive husband with dominant wife, either in "in-search-of-a-mother" or in paranoid patterns.)

2. *Intimacy*

Emotional intimacy (love) and physical intimacy (sensuousness), without intercourse or without response during intercourse.

Wife. "He is a great lover. Foreplay goes on for hours. He uses his hands, mouth and every part of my body. He talks to me and tells me how much he loves me. He sets me up so I am ready for sex. But he doesn't have intercourse with me. He must be afraid of it. I don't know what I will do if he doesn't have intercourse with me." ("In-search-of-a mother" pattern with passive husband.)

Husband. "She is great on kissing and holding and hugging and talking romantically. But she can't respond in intercourse. She can't have an orgasm. I can stimulate her by the hour and she never can let go. I have lost confidence in myself. I would love to have the experience of a woman responding to me. I wonder if I could still do that. I would rather be with a prostitute than with her. She doesn't really love me despite the fact that she is always talking about how much she can love." ("Cold-sick" husband with "love-sick" wife.)

3. No sex (lust); no intimacy—physical (sensuousness) or emotional (love).

This is a relationship maintained by a bond of mutual dependency and hate.

Wife. "On our honeymoon he brought ten books. He doesn't talk to me, he doesn't make love to me, he doesn't have intercourse with me. I have to beg him for intercourse. I think there must be something wrong with me. I am so furious, I think I am going crazy. If I'm not careful in what I say, his feelings get hurt all the time. I wish I had married a truck driver." ("Love-sick" wife with allegedly "cold-sick" husband.)

Husband. "She treats me like dirt. Touching her is like touching an icicle. No talking, no kissing, no sex. I have turned to masturbation and have fantasies of other women. I know I am going to have an affair." (Dependent husband with dominant or paranoid wife.)

RELATING LUST, SENSUOUSNESS, AND LOVE TO THE MARITAL PATTERNS

Sexual Difficulties in the "Love-Sick" Wife and the "Cold-Sick" Husband Pattern

The husbands in this type of marital pattern have difficulty in all three areas—sensuousness, love, and lust. They tend to be mechanical in their lovemaking, although they try to do a "good job" and to prove their sexuality. They experience performance anxiety and may suffer from premature ejaculation, impotence, and avoidance of sex. The wife's seductiveness makes her appear to be interested in genital activities culminating in an orgasm. She is not. She is interested in kissing, holding, hugging (sensuousness); talking and doing things together (emotional intimacy—love), but not in intercourse with orgasm (lust).

With the recent development of sexual dysfunction clinics, recognition that certain sexual dysfunctions occur frequently in particular marriages has been reported in the literature. In this type of marriage, which involves an obsessive-compulsive husband and a hysterical wife, Jacobs (1974) reports two types of problems. Where the wife is capable of orgasm, the husband commonly suffers from premature ejaculation. More often the wives report never having experienced orgasm and are of the primary type of orgasmic dysfunction. They never achieved orgasm through masturbation because of negative meanings attached to sexual pleasures. They approach intercourse with veiled hopes of being mothered, nurtured, cuddled, and caressed. The husbands' "unromantic" approach not only does not gratify their needs but reactivates their long-dormant, near-psychotic anger against their neglecting mothers, which evokes fear of loss of control (psychosis) if they allow themselves to have an orgasm. The husband's previously mentioned expectation that his wife be orgasmic often reflects his need that she be so to prove that she appreciates him, is grateful to him for all that he has given her, and loves him. When these needs are repeatedly thwarted by her inability to be orgasmic, he suffers a narcissistic injury, becomes continuously hostile to her, withdraws his feelings behind a cold front—as he has done since his childhood rejections by his mother—and gives rise to the picture of him which his wife labels "cold-sick" and which psychiatrists label obsessive-compulsive personality.

Sexual Difficulties in the "In-Search-of-a-Mother" Pattern

In the sexual area, these husbands are excellent lovers in terms of sensuousness, with much time spent in foreplay and oral activities. They also stress their needs for emotional intimacy with both the wife and the "other woman." Although the men are usually potent, some even hyperactive in intercourse, there is an element of fragility to their activity in this area. The man needs to prove his potency to insure the woman's support and thus is subject to anxieties that could contribute to premature ejaculation or erective failures when he is fatigued, intoxicated, or overburdened with responsibilities. This is a secondary impotence that tends to perpetuate itself because of hostility held by the husband, who resents his dependence on his wife or the "other woman." He cannot openly express his anger against the woman because of his fear of losing her, so he does it indirectly through impotence. If the husband has a sexual complaint against this type of wife, it is in the area of being low on physical intimacy-sensuousness. She usually has achieved orgasm, being able to lose control over sexual feelings in a situation in which she is dominant. She usually continues responsive in this way until she finds out about the "other woman." At this time she is prone to develop situational orgasmic dysfunction.

Sexual Difficulties in the Dependent-Dependent Pattern

Both partners are lacking in capacity for emotional intimacy-love. Since both are looking for physical intimacy from another person and might be responsive in this area with a strong person, they are unable to enjoy sensuousness with each other. Instead of bringing closeness, sensate focus exercises between these mates may precipitate adverse reactions that disrupt whatever precarious equilibrium is present in the marriage. Intercourse is a disruptive experience since the wives often suffer from primary orgasmic dysfunction and the husbands complete the picture with persistent premature ejaculation indicating weak ego controls.

When these wives get involved in affairs with aggressive men who are not afraid of them, they may show strong sensuous capacities and even become orgasmic. Similarly when these men are involved in affairs where the woman indicates her sexual desires freely and is noncritical of any performance, these men show strong sensuous capacities. Also, freed of fears of rejection and criticism they show greater capacity to prolong erections.

Sexual Difficulties in the Paranoid Pattern

The dynamics of the paranoid personality cause difficulties in the areas of physical and emotional intimacy. The area of intercourse is affected by the mate's need to prove his masculinity, leading to prolonged periods of erection during vaginal containment. However, this pseudopotency is tainted with failure to ejaculate, ejaculatory incompetence, or retarded ejaculation. He also may need the wife to be orgasmic or multiorgasmic to prove his potency. When the wife is in the *folie à deux* attitude toward her husband and capable of losing herself and her ego boundaries to him, she may respond multiorgasmically to his prolonged states of erection. When she begins to separate to fight for herself, or is in a depression, she cannot respond as he so desperately needs her to do. This precipitates rages in her husband with manifestations of pathological jealousy and accusations of infidelity.

When the wife is the paranoid personality, her suspicions and jealousy form an integral part of her attack upon her husband. This causes him to withdraw into a lack of physical and emotional intimacy as well as sexual apathy which gives her more equilibrium. She avoids intimacy of any form to maintain the tenuous boundaries of her self. In this respect she is markedly different from the "love-sick" wife who seeks nurturance from a good mother. The paranoid wife seeks escape from the malignant persecutory imago of her infantile years. This contributes to orgasmic difficulties as well as to episodes of vaginismus.

ELABORATION ON THE THREE ASPECTS OF SEXUALITY

Having presented the clinical material which crystalized out three separate aspects of sexuality and related them to the four psychopathologic marriage patterns, we can now discuss these aspects in greater depth. This will then allow for the derivation of normal values for sexuality in marriage.

Love

Love is such a many splendored thing and subject to so many differing definitions that it is easier to start with what it is not (or pseudo-love).

The "love-sick" wife talks about love and gives love as though it were a thing you dump on another person like some burden which the other person should then appreciate and repay. The "love-sick" wife gives herself as an object to be made happy by the "fortunate" recipient of her gift. Since this type of love tends to be felt as a burden by the other person and engenders resentment, it might be called pathological or regressive love. Its goal seems to be a fusion with the other. It seems to be a return to the original infant-mother relationship where the infant is a burden and is loved for itself, not for what it gives or does. In marked contrast, then, is what we would call mature love. This is not something that can be given. It is analogous to the force in the constant mother in the mother-child relationship. It is a motivating force that allows the individual to give protection, sustenance, peace, pleasure, and stimulus to growth and development of the other person. Anne Morrow Lindbergh (1974) states it beautifully:

> It does seem to me more and more that love has no value in itself or by itself. . . . I don't think it is anything that you can give, or if you can, it is valueless.
>
> Love is a force *in you* that enables you to give *other* things. It is the motivating power. It enables you to give strength and power and freedom and peace to another person. It is not a result; it is a cause. It is not a product; it produces. It is a power, like money or steam or electricity. It is valueless unless you can give something else *by means* of it (p. 231).

To the last sentence I would add: "without requiring anything in return from the other person."

Love is not infatuation. Salzman (1975) distinguishes love from infatuation in the following ways. He clearly emphasizes that infatuation is very self-oriented. It is a wild, ecstatic feeling of having fallen in love or a fantasy about being in love. Because of the excesses, dramatics, and heroics, it often gives the impression of greater devotion than actually exists in mature love. In infatuation, the other person is idealized and viewed as having everything. There is little reciprocity; it is more a form of worship. The other person may be used solely to document one's competence, and this is particularly true of the individual who is forever infatuated with partners and never in love with anyone. Of course, not every loving relation is one of profound, intense, total commitment, but in varying degrees there is some mutual concern and less reliance on self-fostered illusions. It is possible that beyond the superficial traits that make a person the object of one's infatuation there can be deeper qualities which later can contribute to the development of love. Although initially drawn to people by outward characteristics, we later discover deeper qualities that are desired, or we do not discover deeper qualities and may develop hate instead of love.

Salzman defines mature love as a state of being in which the satisfaction or security of another person becomes as important as one's own. This is a true expression of intimacy, tenderness, and collaborative relationship with another human being. For this reason, many people believe that true love develops prior to the maturation of the sexual function and is uncomplicated by lust. As has been shown in the preceding material, and as will be elaborated upon, lust can function separately without infatuation or love. However, when lust is intermingled with infatuation or love, there is an enhancement of each quality, a synergistic effect, which contributes to the difficulties of distinguishing one from the other.

Salzman continues this important differentiation between love and infatuation by stressing that love recognizes the strivings of the other person toward dependency and independency and preserves each partner's integrity as an individual self. It is a relationship of mutual trust and respect, and it allows for the expression of the maximum potentialities of each person for giving and taking. In the state of love there is respect, concern, and affection for the other person and not simply mutual exploitation or mutual satisfaction of needs. As in mature sexual behavior, one does not give and the other get, but both give and receive at the same time. This is not an idealized description of love, but a statement of the possibilities which unfortunately may be rarely achieved. However, it is achieved at times by some lucky people and thus can be validated. Therefore love should not be confused with sentimentality, romantic exhilaration, or simple sado-masochistic dependency.

Love has been defined by Ashley Montagu as "a principal developer of the potentialities for being human and the chief stimulus to the development of social competence. It is created both for the receiver and the giver and can only benefit, create freedom and order" (Montagu, 1962). This formulation adds still another dimension to the understanding of love in a mature sense. Infatuation and romantic love, however, may be the prelude and the precursor for the development of truly loving relationships. Obviously they are not enough, and without the development of love they can disappear in a wave of hatred.

Typical, however, of the paradoxical qualities in human nature are the clinical observations that love and sex are sometimes mutually exclusive. The presence of love may eliminate the possibility of sexual responsiveness. The most clarifying material to come to my attention was at a public lecture on sex when I was handed a written question from the audience with one minute to answer. The question was "what would you offer a woman who has fourteen orgasms with each sexual experience?" Under the circumstances, all I could say was, "May I offer my congratulations," and then turn to the next question. After the program a man came to me and said that he had written the question. His problem was that he had met a recently widowed woman who responded in this way each time they had sexual relations. Her problem was that she broke the record reported by Kinsey and feared she would become a nymphomaniac. It was easy to give reassurance that multiorgasmic responses in women were normal and she need not be worried. But that did not solve his problem. He loved her and wanted to marry her, but she would have no part of him. She had been happily married for many years in a marriage of mutual love and respect. She and her husband had been socially prominent and pillars of the church and community. Although regular intercourse had been a part of their marriage, she had never been orgasmic and had never missed it. They had had four children who had been a great source of mutual pleasure. Her story laid to rest the popular fallacy that if two people love each other sex between them automatically will be enormously satisfying. Her attitude toward her present disappointed suitor was that he was beneath her socially, he would not be a suitable father for her children, and she did not love him. Here the absence of infatuation or love allowed the fullest expression of her previously repressed lust. Deep love does not necessarily ensure good sex, and sex may sometimes be more erotic without love (Lazarus, 1974).

There are degrees of love and different types of love. The quality of love is subjective and differs not only from person to person but also at different times within the same person as to frequency, intensity, duration, and spiritual quality. The emphasis of love in the "love-sick" wife is on great tenderness, compassion, concern, warmth, yearnings and gentleness, while being unresponsive or even negative to passionate, ardent, and vigorous lovemaking. This type of mate (wives or husbands) may concentrate so much on the love and affection that sexual impulses become diffused and result in decreased erotic stimulation. When the two mates are alike in this respect, a harmonious marriage ensues. However, the presence of a loving attitude between partners is not a sufficient requirement for sexual activities. If one of the partners has expectations of sexual responses which the other cannot gratify—and especially if this lack of sexual capacity is misinterpreted as a lack of love—marital difficulty can ensue.

There is an old rubric that a woman needs to feel loved in order to respond sexually and that a man needs to respond sexually in order to feel love. Not only is this male-female differentiation fallacious when applied to any given individual, but a person (male or female) can feel loved and not be able to respond sexually, or can experience a full sexual response without feeling love.

The combinations of love, lust, and sensuousness are so complexly intertwined that marital therapists must be careful neither to accept nor to perpetuate the many common fallacies and value judgments that abound in this area. If not careful about these generalizations the therapist can reinforce unrealistic expectations of either mate that are often incapable of achievement in most marriages.

There is an important aspect of love that is best introduced by the old saying that "love is blind." This recognizes that when a person is "in love," or perhaps is "infatuated," there is a marked overvaluation of the love object and an underestimation or a denial of the deficiencies. In the study of healthy, happy marriages the lover turns out not to have been blind but to have been perceptive of potentialities in the loved one which others had not seen and which the love relationship had developed to their fullest. This searchlight of love might be considered an *other*-fulfilling prophesy."

Another way of understanding that love need not be blind is that mature love shows the capacity to accept the other person *in toto*— good and bad together—as one person who on balance is loved. The capacity for love is in the lover. The capacity to respond to love with growth and development is (or is not) in the one who is loved.

I do not want to leave the love aspect of sexuality without identifying its place in the healthy marriage. A marriage is different from two separate individuals in forming a structure that is greater than the sum of its two parts—the arch. The arch is the interpersonal relationship in the marriage. The following quote from Carl Sandburg (1957) describes it and identifies it as only a creative writer can do:

> The arch never sleeps. When the arch holds, all else holds. Love stands and hangs by an arch. Hate breaks the arch. The rainbow is an arch. Where you find truth, love, harmony and lasting strength, an arch bends and curves over it as a blessing and an oath. Unity, union, you get it only with an arch. Hate and pride break arches. Love and understanding build unbreakable arches (p. 233).

Lust

As illustrated early in this chapter, in one couple a mate may complain bitterly about the other mate being interested in intercourse only, without intimacy. However, this apparently horrible state of affairs is elevated to an ideal state with another couple wherein one mate is so sensitive and gets feelings hurt so easily that sensuousness, lust, and love are all turned off. Lust is a biologic trait which in pure culture is nonaffectional and pleasurable even if no capacity for love and affection is present. Obviously, as in the example given above under love, it is socially influenced, so that it may be expressed under one set of conditions and suppressed and/or repressed under another. In addition, it is influenced by intrapsychic and interpersonal conflicts which weaken the force of the biological drive. Marital therapists are alert to these conflicting forces and work therapeutically to free the drive of these restrictive influences. When therapists have sufficient experience with marriages destroyed by absence of lust in one partner (whether due to physical or psychological causes), they are less apt to be critical or moralistic about sex without love. And though it does not always follow, there are times when one sees newly discovered sex beget love.

Among the widespread cultural stereotypes against which marital therapists must be on guard is the notion that the quality of sex would nearly always be inferior without love and that sex without love is selfish, self-centered, and egotistic (Lazarus, 1974). Contrary to this notion, professional lovers who usually feel no particular love or affection for their partners are often expert, capable lovers, take pride in their sexual mastery and in their ability to satisfy their partners, and are extremely attentive and considerate sexual partners. This is in contrast to many mates who profess love and affection but are insensitive, inconsiderate, and inadequate sex partners.

Sensuousness

A wave of emphasis on the development of sensuous feelings has swept America as an aid towards developing (or perhaps as a substitute for) intimacy. Modern sex therapists have taught sensual and sexual stimulation by fondling, caressing, massaging, kissing (sensate focus) to promote the recognition and acceptance of experiencing new forms of pleasurable body feelings (Schimel, 1975). Although this sensual explosion was set off by the pioneering work of Masters and Johnson, it has sometimes been pulled out of the context of their work. In this national phenomenon, the use of sensate focus is for the purpose of a sexual turn-on. Masters and Johnson's use of the sensate focus was for the purpose of having the active partner develop sensual responsibility, to neutralize his or her fear of performance. The person who was being touched was not to allow the touches to go too far, in order to enhance the natural process of the partner's sexual drive. However, the change of the original intent is validated by the natural need of the recipient for this form of loving, care, stimulation, and preparation.

The sensuous aspects of sex and intercourse are difficult to separate from the emotional elements. However, they do contain mechanical and technical skills that grow out of experience and one's orientation to pleasure and which are not directly related to the attitude toward the mate (Lazarus, 1974). Technique is more important here, and the marital therapist can read the numerous books now available (Kaplan, 1974), as well as obtain training in this area for those marriages in which such therapy is indicated.

It might be well to state briefly at this point the relationship between marital therapy and sex therapy. The goal of marital therapy is to foster the growth of each mate by harnessing the forces within the marriage. It is difficult in clinical practice to make a clear distinction between sex therapy and marriage therapy because 75 percent of the patients have both marital discord and sexual problems. Sexual aspects are but strands in the marital relationship which, when frayed, may need to be reinforced along with the other, nonsexual aspects that are frayed. Sometimes repairing the other strands repairs the sexual strands and vice versa.

When sexual dysfunction causes marital discord, sex therapy is indicated. When marital discord impairs sexual functioning, one or both types of therapy can be used. Severe marital discord precludes immediate sex therapy and is an indication for marital therapy.

Schimel (1975) makes a telling point in warning about the danger of an overly mechanical approach during the proper and loving preparation of each partner by the other. He describes how modern sex books and practices give detailed descriptions of approved modes of fondling. There is a stress on "the proper," such as properly respectful, if not reverential, attitudes which are to be communicated in the course of lovemaking, as well as proper timing, the practice of which actually promotes withholding by one partner until the other reaches an optimal level of sexual excitement and, presumably, makes mutually satisfying orgasm possible. Schimel's point can be called, "What ever happened to impetuous love?"; or "Abandon may be more erotic than following a sexual game plan."

The aspect of sensuousness has been invaded by techniques. Techniques have advantages and disadvantages. They have no magical powers. This is illustrated by clinical material such as in Schimel's case where a male patient stated that he had become a much better lover since he stopped thinking about how to please his wife and that she had now found him more exciting.

The outstanding contributions and effectiveness of sex therapy do not obviate the importance to marital therapy of such pleasurable qualities in an interpersonal relationship as joy, laughter, play, playfulness, preference, appetite, or desire. There is a currently popular game which throws this problem into bold relief. It is called the

"Island Game." The player is presented with a name of another person and asked: "If you were alone on a deserted island with . . . . . . (insert name) how long would it take you to 'make out' with this person?" The wide variation of responses, ranging from "seconds" to "weeks" to "no way," is revealing of the difference between mechanics and desire.

DERIVATION OF NORMAL SEXUAL VALUES

From the above pathology we can derive a picture of sexual normality: an individual who can combine the pleasures of emotional and physical intimacy together with the pleasure of adequate intercourse. This is an adult who has triumphed against the odds and emerged a winner. Apparently it is a rare breed. It does not happen as often as we wish it would, but it is at least an ideal, a goal to be achieved. But again a note of warning: These are reference points, guidelines only. They are to be used with discretion. Care must be taken not to set up new expectations or tyrannical standards that create unrealistic demands with resulting guilt, anxiety, and loss of spontaneous responses.

VARIATION FROM NORMAL VALUES IN STABLE MARRIAGES

An ideal marriage from the sexual standpoint would be a matching up of two individuals who fit the picture of sexual normality described above by combining the pleasures of all three aspects of sexuality in their relationship. But what of those who have not achieved the ideal? Adequate matchups still occur in nature whether by choice or by chance. These are not the ones who complain. They are not the ones who come for marital therapy. They also are referred to in the material of those who come for marital therapy. The following are some example of less than ideal but workable couplings.

Lust Minus Sensuousness and Love

A highly (intercourse-minded) sexual male lacking in capacity for emotional or physical intimacy is married to a woman with the same combination. The sexual union appears to be the bond that keeps them together. They may fight and scream at one another all day long, but it doesn't interfere with their bedtime union which keeps the marriage palatable. This indicates either a capacity to isolate intercourse from the other two areas or a tendency to regard combative behavior as a normal part of discourse and not as aggressive behavior intended to injure. In some marriages, such behavior, even if escalated to the point of physical aggression, is defined within boundaries of love and discourse.

Sensuousness and Love Minus Lust

A husband and wife are affectionate, loving, considerate of one another all day long but not strongly motivated for and during intercourse. His quickness to ejaculate doesn't bother her since it keeps him happy and she knows she will not respond anyhow, and he doesn't expect a response from her which she feels incapable of experiencing. When vital needs are few and expectations are low, harmony is easily achieved. This combination does not need treatment. If they seek help because of anxiety aroused by mass media emphasis on what they should expect in order to be "normal," reassurance is sufficient.

Low Sensuousness, Lust and Love

A low intimacy and low sex life marital pair has a low key approach which results in what may appear to be a cold marriage but one which is workable for them. Needs and expectations are minimal. They appear to be like Grant Wood's American Gothic portrait, but appreciation of one another is high. It is like *folie à deux* without the *folie.*

Conclusions

What valid conclusions can be made from this material drawn from less than ideal but functioning, stable marriages? In effect these marriages are working with fewer functional areas than some of the pathological marriages illustrated earlier in this chapter; yet, even with minimal dovetailing of needs between the mates, these marriages remain stable and reasonably harmonious. The generalization can be drawn (validated by clinical experience) that marital disharmony is a manifestation of dis-ease between two human beings in the marital relationship. The dis-ease is a result of expectations in one or both partners which are not gratified by the other. Where expectations are mutually gratified, health results. Where expectations and disappointments are few, functional marriages with an absence of dis-ease result.

Thus the problem of avoiding dis-ease in marriage is one of proper matching up of couples prior to marriage. The problem of producing a harmonious marriage is one of adjusting expectations during the marriage. This involves an understanding of the marriage contract which is dealt with in the next chapter. The material from this section allows for a proper emphasis on variations from the ideal and stable marriages based on the basic necessities.

REFERENCES

Jacobs, L. I. (1974), Sexual problems and personalities in four types of marriage. *Medical Aspects of Human Sexuality*, 8: 160-181.

Kaplan, H. S. (1974), *The New Sex Therapy*, New York: Brunner/Mazel.

Lazarus, A. A. (1974), Sex with (and without) love. *Medical Aspects of Human Sexuality*, 8, 12: 32-42.

Lindbergh, A. (1974), *Locked Rooms and Open Doors: Diaries and Letters of Anne Morrow Lindbergh, 1933-1935*. New York: Harcourt, Brace Jovanovich, p. 231.

Montagu, A. (1962), *The Humanization of Man*. New York: Grove Press.

Salzman, R. (1975), Discussion. *Medical Aspects of Human Sexuality*, February, p. 108.

Sandburg, C. (1957), "Remembrance Rock." In *The Sandburg Range*. New York: Harcourt, Brace and Co., p. 233.

Schimel, J. L. (1975), Impetuous Love. *Medical Aspects of Human Sexuality*, 9, 3: 94-110.

4

The Marriage Contract

AN UNDERSTANDING of the marriage contract contributes to (1) shaping the initial diagnostic interviews, (2) clarifying the therapeutic contract each partner is likely to make with the therapist and (3) illustrating one of the techniques of marital therapy. Elaboration of each of these aspects will be presented in later chapters.

In the preceding chapters, normal values for marriage were derived from clinical material of psychopathological marriages. This led to the recognition that marital disharmony is a manifestation of dis-ease in a relationship that results from the absence of one or more solid, constant, mutually gratified expectations capable of overcoming the ungratified expectations in either mate or both.

Where important and sufficient expectations are mutually gratified, marital harmony results. This principle leads directly to the subject of the marriage contract.

The marriage contract is not only a formal (written or spoken) declaration of what can be expected by each mate from the other but too often an unspoken set of conscious expectations. In addition, each mate harbors an unknown (unconscious) and therefore unacknowledgeable set of expectations for the other. A marriage contract through which sufficient expectations are mutually gratified results in marital harmony.

A solid initial contract is the greatest guarantee of marital harmony. Although contracts do have to be renegotiated during the life cycle of a marriage, such renegotiations are extremely painful experiences for most couples. Even when successfully renegotiated, they leave nuclei of bitterness, easily reawakened by further disappointments.

Behaviorists define contracting as writing down specific expected behaviors and then reinforcing arrangements that are agreed upon by two or more persons involved (Patterson, 1971). It is a means of being specific and is also a commitment. It is noteworthy that recent behavioral science literature illustrates marked increase of interest in personal marriage contracts—an age-old ingredient of marriages whose importance has been neglected. This re-emergence of interest in the marriage contract is not just old wine in new bottles. A new ingredient has been added: the understanding of the unspoken, unconscious contract in intimate interpersonal relationships. The way in which a contract is written, as well as the content, reveals the underlying intent. The new scientific interest in such contracts may be a reflection of the many changes in current marriage and family life, one of them being the personal contract that many couples, married and unmarried, are drawing up between themselves, even to the point of writing their own marriage ceremony.

Historically, the personal marriage contract has been an essential feature of many cultures. The *ketubah*, the ancient Jewish marriage contract, testified to the legitimacy of the marital relation under Talmudic law. It established guarantees, mostly economic, and set forth obligations of husband and wife to each other. Jewish contracts concerning marriage were so important to the culture that a custom developed, popularly referred to as *tenaim*, which were the conditions agreed upon in *planning* a forthcoming wedding. The term technically meant "conditions." The general reference was to some form of contract where conditions are set forth forming the obligations of two parties. In early societies, kin or clan determined not only the definition of the married state but also how individuals were to go about the business of becoming and remaining married. The signing of such a contract of conditions, the *tenaim*, was like a formal engagement. The conditions included things like date and place of the marriage, virginity of the bride, and financial obligations binding upon both the bride and groom and their respective parents in financing the wedding and providing for the newly married couple. These conditions were a safeguard for the woman's elementary human rights and indicated a culture where mutual obligations were defined.

That economic responsibilities were at stake should not be underestimated. It is important to understand that a greater psychological depth is involved in such matters than merely dealing with the practicalities or, as might be considered in our romantic culture, the mundane aspect of money. How a person deals with money provides an important insight into his character structure, value system, unconscious needs, and interpersonal relationships. If these qualities mesh between the parties involved so that a contract is established to which a genuine commitment can be made, the odds for a harmonious marriage based on gratification of expectations are good.

The *tenaim* contract usually carried a penalty clause in the event the conditions were not met. The contract was so binding and the release from it so difficult that rabbis advised a divorce after the wedding instead of a breach of this contract by not having the wedding take place. Such intense external pressures to discharge one's obligations and to maintain marriages are not present in our American culture.

As societies developed, the church and the state rather than kin or clan took control of such personal matters as marriage and divorce. Some of the old provisions became laws of the state. The current revival of personalized marriage contracts is a renewal of an old practice but with a shift from church or clan to control by the responsible individuals who are fashioning their own personal lives. Fascinating but as yet unpublished research is being done in the area of collecting and studying current personal marriage contracts by the Institute on the Family and the Bureaucratic Society in the Department of Sociology at Case Western Reserve University. It will be interesting to follow such studies and see whether the responsible individuals making their contracts will do better than those with contracts made by clans and early societies.

Can "nuclear" contracts succeed without the reinforcement of "extended" contracts? From brief clinical experience, with of course small numbers, we are already seeing instances where such personally written contracts still contain (1) dishonest conscious contracts, (2) lack of awareness of unconscious needs not met by the contracts, or (3) both of the above. The complexity of human nature predicts that the new approach will have advantages and disadvantages but will not necessarily be a significantly better method. It will be interesting to see if this prediction holds true. Premarital counseling offers a couple an opportunity for writing a lasting and flexible initial contract.

The Institute on the Family and the Bureaucratic Society calls the personal contract a new form of marriage bond. Preliminary work indicates that contracts have one or more of the following provisions: (1) division of household labor, (2) use of living space, (3) each partner's responsibility for child rearing and socialization, (4) property, debts, living expenses, (5) career commitment and legal domicile, (6) rights of inheritance, (7) use of surnames, (8) range of permissible relations with others, (9) obligations of the marital dyad in various life sectors such as work, leisure, community, and social life, (10) grounds for splitting or divorce, (11) initial and subsequent contract periods and negotiability, (12) sexual fidelity vs. relationships beyond the partnership and (13) position regarding procreation or adoption of children.

CLINICAL ILLUSTRATIONS

Clinical experience shows that the marriage contract involves a conscious and an unconscious set of terms. When the conscious and unconscious expectations of mates mesh, marital harmony is assured. When the conscious contract is understood and agreed upon by both partners but there is an unconscious disagreement with it by one or both partners, dis-ease results.

The only recent recognition of the importance of contracts lies in the early psychotherapeutic emphasis on the individual and intrapsychic conflicts. With the shift in focus in the fifties to transactional aspects of relationships and more recently to the development of behavior therapy, the recognition of the significance of contracts between persons followed naturally.

The influence of contracts can be clearly seen in the types of marriages described in the previous chapter. In one of the couples of the "Love-Sick" Wife and the "Cold-Sick" Husband marriage pattern, the following contractual conditions existed:

The wife was an attractive, bright, vivacious, romantic, active and fun-loving person. She was an excellent talker, brightening a room full of people with her conversation, but at times extremely opinionated. The latter quality might cause embarrassing social situations but things were never dull. As in this marriage pattern, she was an hysterical personality whose outgoing presentation covered up many fears and anxieties. In childhood, she had a school phobia. In adulthood she had many shifting fears such as fear of flying, fear of cancer, fear of dying. Despite her fears, in other areas she showed counterphobic mechanisms and exposed herself to dangerous situations (driving rapidly, walking alone at late hours in dangerous neighborhoods) which made her appear fearless. She would operate at a feverish pitch, involved in so many activities that she would appear to be an extraordinary achiever, and then suddenly collapse into tears and feelings of weakness and inadequacy. She would then quickly cover up these episodes, minimize their significance, and start the cycle over. Her school record was a source of shame to her. Though bright and quick in her thinking, she was not a worker. If she could grasp a problem quickly and solve it, she was all right. If it took concentration, and attention and involved frustration and prolonged work, she avoided it. She only wanted to know the answers to problems in mathematics (at which she did poorly); she did not want to be bothered with understanding how to solve them. She needed constant approval from others in order to function well. In the presence of disapproval or indifference she became furious or withdrew.

The husband was a handsome, personable individual with an appearance of boyishness. He was slow, did not grasp social situations quickly, did not speak much or when he did would often be exposed as having missed the point. He was not a "natural" like his wife. He was a plodder. Given a problem (as in mathematics), he would stay with it for prolonged periods of time until he understood how it worked and how to solve similar problems. He often did not know what he wanted to do, but once pointed in a direction (even in the choice of his career) he plodded his way through to success.

When they met in their late teens, she instantly knew what she wanted. She was physically attracted to him and she wanted him. She was not going on to college, since it was beyond her work capacity. She was not going to develop her artistic ability since it also required work. And of course, she not only felt that menial jobs were beneath her, she couldn't hold one. He was to be the solution of all her problems.

He didn't know what he wanted. He was not ready for marriage but he knew that a man was supposed to get married. After being manipulated sufficiently, he did what he was supposed to do. He knew that she was "cute." Her physical attractiveness was not that important to him personally though it would look good to others. She convinced him that marriage was not only the right thing to do but that it would be "good" for him. She would take care of all the social arrangements and, by her talking, carry things off successfully for both of them. Also, she held out the promise that when they had intercourse, after marriage of course, he would find her to be as sexy as she appeared to be.

The conscious contract made between the two of them was that she would take care of running the house, of all the social arrangements, and be sexual, and that he would do his work and provide the means for purchase of a home, clothes, and rearing of the children. The arrangement was that if he did what she wanted (get married), she would then do what he wanted. The unspoken conscious contract she made was that, in return for taking care of his needs (for example, preparing food according to his idiosyncracies), he would change his indifferent personality and love her romantically as she needed to be loved. In exchange for her guidance and direction in the "right" path he would admire her, adore her, and love her. Her contract illustrated her dishonesty.

His unspoken contract incorporated his parents' pattern and advice to him: never let your mate know what your true financial resources are. In effect, don't trust your wife. His unspoken contract was that she would remain the flighty scatterbrain she appeared to be with money, would not know what he was doing with money, and would not be financially demanding, enabling him to achieve financial security. She was to be grateful for what he gave her and was not to make demands upon him that would interfere with his goals.

In short, she planned to do everything for him so he would give her the love, closeness, and intimacy on which she thrived, and he planned to give her the basic economic requirements for which she was to be grateful and make no further demands.

The unconscious contracts shed further light on this marriage, which was destined for failure. Those aspects of the marriage contract which are not accessible to conscious awareness may be regarded, for clinical purposes, as working hypotheses inferred from the behavior, fantasies, and other productions of each spouse. Here, dreams are indeed the road to the unconscious portion of the marital contract. The wife had a dream during treatment of a puking, crying baby, terrified at being abandoned and alone. This was a repetition of her original relationship with her mother who had to leave her to go to work because the inadequate father could not earn a living for the family. The patient married a man who she consciously knew would be a solid provider in contrast to her father and whom she unconsciously expected to accept her terrors and fears and cure her by loving her in the way she had not been loved by a harried and absent mother. When he did not "mother" her but coldly rejected her for demanding time and attention, she went into episodes of uncontrolled rage, attacking him unmercifully. Her unconscious contract was that he would not hate her for this. When he remained "cold," she collapsed and experienced a return of her incapacitating childhood fears.

The husband's unconscious contract was that he would do many of the things demanded of him by his wife even though he did not want to do them and then could feel hurt and angry that she did not let him do what he wanted to do. He thereafter felt righteously angry at her lack of awareness of his needs and could remain secretive about his financial activities. This was a repetition of his early relationship with his mother who had been a cold, rejecting woman. Her hatred of her husband caused her to reject and ignore the needs of this boy who was the youngest and the unwanted child in the family. He responded to his wife's needs and demands for love with the same coldness and rejection of his childhood needs shown by his hated mother. In summary he had a contract partly conscious and partly unconscious: he would do what the other person wanted even though he did not want to do it (such as getting married) and in return would expect appreciation. When his sacrifice was not appreciated, he would then become hurt, coldly angry, and withdrawn. When told what to do, he dutifully followed the letter of the law, missed the spirit of the law (love and intimacy in a marriage relationship), and lived with chronic hurt and anger as a silently reproachful martyr, free to do as he wished.

The wife, needing love desperately, presented herself to her husband to be cared for, with an expectation of immediate response. What she received was a cold hatred, which made her feel either bewildered, guilty, unlovable, and depressed, or ashamed of being inadequate to make him love her. It was clear from her overwhelming anxieties and phobic symptoms that she was sicker than he was. She was overwhelmed by her emotions; he was not by his. However, she judged sickness not by work capacity but by one's capacity to love (as she defined it, presenting oneself to be loved by the other person) and thus declared him to be sicker than she was—The "Love-Sick" Wife and the "Cold-Sick" Husband. Her contract was to love and not work (be taken care of). His contract was to work and not love (avoidance of intimacy). She was overwhelmed by the responsibilities of standing alone (work); he felt overwhelmed by the flood of emotions demanded in a reciprocal response of intimacy. He withdrew because he experienced intimacy as a loss of his self, his freedom, and his independence.

All of these responses, conscious and unconscious, operate simultaneously on different levels. In action they fuse into a whole whose original chords are difficult to distinguish in seemingly unimportant events. For example, in the couple above whose contract was dissected into its component parts, the following vignette was first presented by the husband. He came home and sat down to dinner with his wife. He noticed that the catsup was missing from the able. In order "not to bother her," he got up to get it. With hatred blazing from her eyes she asked him what he wanted. He felt that there was no good reason for her hatred. He felt that he could not stand having her talk to him as if he were "a dog." He hated her, felt hurt, and righteous.

When such a picture is presented in individual therapy, it is very difficult to unravel the threads and to clarify the conscious and unconscious interplay between the mates. It is also difficult to clarify the intrapsychic problem when the individual is defending it behind the screen of the disturbed interpersonal relationship. Even if the therapist is capable of penetrating the fog and reconstructs and interprets the missing pieces, it does not have the impact of the other mate's presence.

In the foregoing example, from my knowledge of their marriage, I was able to tease order out of the pieces and confront the husband with the facts that his wife had gone to extremes in preparing a perfect dinner with an abundance of his favorite foods prepared exactly the way he liked them. She was trying to please him, to gain recognition and love. He was oblivious to the fact that she was trying so hard to please him. He made no comment at the obvious feast placed in front of him. His getting up from the table to do something himself was to her a rejection. She knew that he was rejecting her and hated him. He did not understand her reaction and hated her for hating him. Without thinking in such terms, each one had violated the marriage contract as the other person defined it. There was no one contract that they both understood and to which they agreed.

When the wife was seen, the above reconstruction was confirmed. Having clarified and acknowledged the interpersonal conflict, it was then possible to work on her intrapsychic conflict. She had to recognize that she was basically terrified to be on her own. She therefore became superpossessive of her husband and tried to control him. She felt he was responsible for keeping her happy. His leaving the table raised her fear of not possessing him despite her intense efforts. She reacted to her terror and her hurt once again with devastating rage, even though he was only reacting in his typical manner, as he had on hundreds of occasions, even before the marriage. She was able to admit that when she saw by his actions that she had to be on her own, she went "crazy." To her, he had violated her contract that if she did everything to please him, he would love her and save her from insanity. To him, she had violated his contract that if he provided economic security, she would be appreciative and make no demands of intimacy. She desired and was comfortable in the symbiotic position and feared autism. He was comfortable in the autistic position and feared symbiosis. She wished to fuse, which she experienced as love—being at one with the other person. He experienced intimacy not as being at one with the other person but as a loss of self, a loss of freedom, a danger of being helplessly sucked back into the womb. These are the depths at which marital therapy must at times work in attempting to forge a working marriage contract between two such different people where there is no original dovetailing of needs.

FORMULATIONS ABOUT THE MARRIAGE CONTRACT

While I was developing my concept of the marriage contract as a useful clinical tool for the clarification and treatment of marital disharmony (Martin, 1970), a landmark article along identical lines of thought emerged from the Marriage Research Committee of the Society of Medical Psychoanalysts, (Sager, et al., 1971). They also use the concept of the marriage contract to understand the interactions between marital partners in terms of congruence or conflict of the partners' reciprocal expectations and obligations. They found these "contractual dynamics" to be powerful determinants of the individuals' behavior, as well as of the quality of the marital relationship. This is because both intrapsychic and transactional factors are important aspects of marital dynamics.

They used the term "marriage contract" to refer to the individual's expressed and unexpressed, conscious and unconscious, concepts of his or her obligations within the marital relationship and to the benefits that he or she expects to derive from the marriage in general and from the mate in particular. But what they so correctly emphasize, above all, is the reciprocal aspect of the contract: that which each partner expects to receive from the spouse in exchange.

Recently Sager has stated (1975):

> "Marriage Contract" is a misnomer as I use the term because I am not referring to formal contracts. These are not legally written contracts or agreements that both mates write out and subscribe to openly. Each spouse has their own "contract" that differs from that of the other. Each person's "contract" or set of expectations is largely unformulated in their own minds or is beyond their own awareness. An individual's "contract" may be internally inconsistent because that person simultaneously may have strong contradictory wishes or needs. For example, one may

have the desire to be independent and yet at the same time require their spouse's approval of their actions.

Sager and his group (1971) also emphasized that while terms of the marriage contract are determined by deep needs that the individual expects the marital relationship to fulfill (healthy, realistic ones as well as neurotic and conflictual ones), two additional factors must be understood. One is that the individual is usually not aware that attempts to fulfill the partner's needs are based on the covert assumption that his own wishes will be fulfilled thereby. In addition the individual is usually not aware of the implicit expectations of his mate. Obviously, then, when significant aspects of the contract cannot possibly be fulfilled, the disappointed partner may react with hurt, rage, neurotic or psychotic symptoms, depression, and psychosomatic symptoms, as if a real agreement had been broken. Being unaware of the partner's expectations, a mate is likely to believe that his or her own obligations had been fulfilled and that the spouse's failure was therefore unfair. It is often impossible to explain to such mates that their expectations are doomed to disappointment because they are based on fantasies that no relationship can fulfill in reality.

Sager and his co-workers (1971) have presented a schematic model of the marriage contract, which is described in detail on the following pages.

Schematic Model of the Marriage Contract

I. *Conscious, Verbalized*

This level refers to what each partner tells the mate about his expectations in clearly understandable language. The reciprocal aspects of these expectations are usually not verbalized or recognized. Surprisingly, when some individuals get married they do not know and cannot verbalize what they expect from marriage. They are happy to sign formalized marriage contracts or accept what the future mate tells them that they expect in marriage. It is only after experience in marriage that their own expectations crystallize.

II. *Conscious, But Not Verbalized*

Here we have each partner's expectations, plans, beliefs, fantasies, etc., which may differ from the content at level I only in that they are not verbalized to the mate, usually because of the fear or shame connected with their disclosure. (Some individuals do not say what they mean or do not mean what they say. The conscious verbalized expectations are merely for the purpose of getting the other person into the marriage. Once the marriage is accomplished, all previous conscious, verbalized expectations are cancelled and new honest ones are expressed. These new ones may be ones that the mate refuses to gratify or finds it impossible to fulfill. For example, a previously penurious, penny-pinching man is suddenly expected to be happy to supply his wife with unlimited financial resources.)

III. *Beyond Awareness*

Level III comprises those desires or needs, often contradictory and unrealistic, of which the partner has no awareness. These may be similar to or in conflict with the needs and expectations operative at levels I and II, depending on how well integrated the individual is.

No matter how congruous contracts may be at the time of marriage, or even for a few years after marriage, contracts on any or all levels are dynamic and may change at any point in each individual's maturational pattern. I have sharply in mind the example of one couple who were extremely happy in the first two years of marriage. His need for extreme, continuous intimacy was a delight to her. It made up for her deprived childhood. In a few years she had her fill of it. She was a naturally creative individual who now wanted some freedom to "do her own thing." He could not stand the separation and disharmony that now erupted in the previously ideal marriage where needs had dovetailed perfectly. Such changes may take place whenever a new force (such as the birth of a baby, a promotion to a higher position for a husband or wife, etc.) enters the marital system.

Since some change during an individual's lifetime is inevitable, the surprise is in observing expectations at the beginning of marriage that the original contract will continue without modification "until death do us part." Even more surprising is to see marriages continue for years with no adaptations to current changes and no changes in the original contract even though it is not working. The only certainty is change, and yet change within people, which is the basis of psychotherapy and the focus of this book, is continuously resisted by the conservative aspect of human nature which is present in varying intensity in every individual.

MISMATING

The subject of the marriage contract leads to the associated issue of mismating (Scanzoni and Scanzoni, 1974). Marital conflicts do not necessarily indicate mismating. However, it is true that some people actually do marry the wrong partners—persons totally unsuited to them.

Genuine mismating is not an infrequently observed phenomenon. Our rising divorce rates attest to the use of this solution for such mismating. To better understand mismating, it is important to recognize *observed* mismating as different from *experienced* mismating; this distinction is critical.

Observed mismating can be seen in pre-engaged couples and also in unmarried cohabitants. The level of conflict is high and, when brought to their attention, a recognition of serious differences is acknowledged. Yet they do not experience the relationship as a mismatch. Even if told that they should not marry before receiving therapy, they usually do marry. Or, if they enter therapy which confirms their incompatibility, they often marry anyway. To understand this phenomenon is to emphasize once again the dovetailing of needs. There is some deeper emotional need which binds them together. For example, they may be alike in feeling that no one else would want them and that marriage to the other person, no matter how disturbing, is better than being alone. Thus they do not *experience* the *observed* mismating. These marriages often develop into a permanent, conflict-habituated marital syndrome. Some situations are irremediable and perpetuation of the relationship is more destructive than therapeutic. These marriages may later lead to divorce or may lead to prolonged psychotherapy with the emergence of the devitalized, apathetic syndrome in the relationship.

It is very difficult for involved mates and often for therapists to recognize that some situations are irremediable and that perpetuation of the relationship is more destructive than therapeutic. The course of events will in part be determined by the goal. If endurance is the goal and the concept of mental health revolves around a capacity to endure, mismating may be perpetuated. If fulfillment, growth, or actualization of the self is the goal and the concept of mental health revolves around these ideals, then perpetuation of the relationship loses its importance.

Genuine mismating can be classified into (1) initial mismating, (2) subsequent mismating, and (3) current mismating. An example of *initial mismating* has just been given. A different example of this type of mismating is illustrated by the fact that some people do not say what they really mean, in order to trick the other person into marriage. A bizarre example is the boy who wanted to marry a beautiful, talented, wealthy girl who was also deeply religious. He professed identical values, but after the marriage told her he really was an atheist. He expected her to accept him as such. It was a genuine mismatch. She not only valued religious convictions but also honesty. Her dilemma was divorce in spite of her religion or living forever in an empty marriage.

Subsequent mismating is the most common toxic process in marital disharmony. As shown in the section on the "Love-Sick" Wife and the "Cold-Sick" Husband, differential growth is the dynamic factor. When both mates grow as individuals, even in different directions (e.g., one in the arts, the other in business), they can respect one another. It is when one continuously grows and the other does not that the gap is almost insurmountable, since differential growth is cumulative and the differences seem to escalate in almost geometrical progression (Cuber, 1974).

Current mismating is the definition the mates themselves give. Again there is a subjective and an objective aspect to the presentation. Usually the subjective aspect of current mismating is how each mate feels the other had failed to make the change which would solve the marital problems. The objective aspect involves the therapist's observation that either or both of the mates have failed to grow as individuals capable of either solving the marital disorder or recognizing it to be unsolvable and dissolving the mismatch. This is the observation of the current intrapsychic status. In addition, current mismating involves the inability of the marital pair to commit themselves to a new marital contract which would effect a viable and vital marriage relationship. This involves both intrapsychic and interpersonal relationship inadequacies.

In the chapters on psychotherapy of clinical entities and techniques of psychotherapy, I will return to utilization of the contract as an aid to solving conflicts. The reader may want to consult some of the extensive literature being published in this area (Burger, 1973; Blechman, 1974; and Weiss, et al., 1974).

REFERENCES

Blechman, E. A. (1974), The family contract game. *The Family Coordinator*, 23, 4: 269-281.

Burger, Robert E. (1973), *The Love Contract*. New York: Van Nostrand Reinhold.

Cuber, J. F. (1974), Commentary. *Medical Aspects of Human Sexuality*, 8, 4: 28-34.

Martin, P. A. (1970), An Historical Survey of Psychotherapy of Marriage Partners. In *Hope: Psychiatry's Commitment*. New York: Brunner/Mazel.

Patterson, G. R. (1971), *Families*. Champaign, Illinois: Research Press Co.

Sager, C. J. (1975), Some information re "marriage contracts" for videotape presentation. Annual Meeting of the American Psychiatric Association, Anaheim, California, May 8, 1975 (Unpublished).

Sager, C. J., Kaplan, H. S., Gundlach, R. H., Kremer, M., Lenz, R., and Royce, J. R. (1971), The marriage contract. *Family Process*, 10, 3: 311-326.

Scanzoni, L. and Scanzoni, J. (1974), Mismating. *Medical Aspects of Human Sexuality*, 8, 4: 8-26.

Weiss, R. L., Birchler, G. R., and Vincent, J. P. (1974), Contractual models for negotiation training in marital dyads. *Journal of Marriage and the Family*, 36, 2: 321-330.

5

Initial Diagnostic Interviews

JUST AS IT IS DIFFICULT to define marital therapy, so it is difficult to designate one type of approach to the initial diagnostic interviews for marital therapy. I use the plural because it is rare that an adequate history and psychological examination can be performed in one interview. It usually takes one or more interviews with each mate and one or more together (if the conjoint interviewing technique is to be used) in order to gather the material necessary for a proper assessment of the mates and the marriage. Such assessment is vital to determining whether marital therapy is indicated and, if so, which of the several types of approaches would best suit the needs of the couple being evaluated. Also, continuing reassessment throughout therapy is necessary as new and sometimes surprising developments dictate a change in diagnosis and in technique.

There are wide variations in the first interview. Sometimes only one mate will be seen; sometimes both mates will be seen immediately and continued as such with no individual interviews (Williams, 1974); sometimes there will be variations between initial individual interviews followed by conjoint interviews with no fixed pattern thereafter, or in reverse order. The decision is sometimes dictated by the mates and at other times by the preferences of the therapists, which vary greatly.

The method and content of the initial interview will vary from one therapist to another. Behavior therapists focus in the first hour primarily on the measurable and potentially measurable behaviors of their clients. They will attempt to identify the behaviors that produce happiness, delineating the conditions that influence these behaviors and systematically structuring the environmental contingencies of which these behaviors are a function (Knox, 1971).

The marital therapist who believes the *marriage* is the patient will take a history that focuses on the difficulties in the marriage and on the interpersonal relationship. Therapists who are primarily interested in the individuals' growth and development within the marriage will include observations of each mate's character and intrapsychic functioning. Thus to the latter a clear understanding of psychopathology and psychodynamics would be the foundation of the initial interviews. To the existentialist or Gestalt therapist, the here and now of the marriage would be the emphasis of the interview.

It is also to be noted that some therapists do not conduct an initial diagnostic interview. Some therapists dispense with diagnostic procedures and start treatment, whatever the problem may turn out to be. Others stress that an artificial distinction between diagnostic and therapeutic interviews is frequently made (MacKinnon and Michels, 1971) and that if there is a single mark of a successful interview, it is the degree to which the patient and therapist develop a shared feeling of understanding. They emphasize that an interview centered on understanding the patient provides more valuable diagnostic information than one which seeks to elicit psychopathology. Although this does not uniformly hold true, it is an important caveat for interviewing. In keeping with this emphasis, it is worth noting that a truly therapeutic interaction is possible in a single session, even though that session be the initial interview (Spoerl, 1975).

In sharp contrast to stressing psychotherapy from the first interview is the position of Howells (Howells, 1975). He castigates the avoidance of diagnosis and emphasizes the danger of plunging in without prior examination. He advocates a return to systematic inquiry as the sure road to knowledge and to being systematic in the clinical field. His dictum is that diagnosis must come before therapy.

I would like to comment at this point on the idea of treatment starting with the initial interview. Although understanding the intent of the therapist to present a therapeutic ambience conducive to the patient's responding positively, I think that such an emphasis is misleading. It overemphasizes that what the therapist does determines whether a therapeutic involvement ensues. One of the aspects of the initial diagnostic interview is to determine whether the patient is capable of entering into a therapeutic relationship which involves change in the patient. The "love-sick" wife is a particularly good example of what appears to be an immediate entry into treatment. Experience often shows, sometimes only many years later, that no change has taken place and that the patient never "entered" treatment and never grasped the concept of an internal change.

Sometimes for the therapist not to "start treatment" in the first hour has a salutary effect on certain patients. These are patients who regress easily in such a milieu and may develop an early psychosis under such conditions. They may feel more comfortable with a diagnostic emphasis as compared to an early intimacy they cannot handle. Thus again there are advantages and disadvantages to each approach. Flexibility and judicious application of knowledge pertinent to each individual situation is more efficacious than global pronouncements about one technique.

Throughout this book I have endeavored to present an overview of the field of marital therapy without espousing one type of approach above another, attempting to avoid polemics or claims of superiority of one approach to another. It would be impractical, however, to describe the many different types of initial diagnostic interviews in this chapter. I will depend therefore upon the presentation of two markedly different approaches.

One is my own approach to the initial diagnostic interview, which follows from the preceding preparatory chapters. I wish again to stress flexibility and selectivity of approach to suit the presenting couple rather than imposition upon every couple of the same routine approach.

The other approach to the initial hours differs greatly in formulation and technique from my own. It is a brief type of interview designed to clear up long waiting lists, to initiate brief therapy where time and resources are limited and where the problem does not involve a change in the individual personality structure of one or both of the partners (Williams, 1974).

My usual approach is based on the recognition of (1) the necessity for a proper assessment of the patient and his situation before embarking on any form of psychotherapy, and (2) continuing reassessment throughout. The initial interview starts with the first contact, perhaps by telephone. It is important to observe which mate called, under what circumstances, and to inquire into why this happened. Many mates call in order to bring the other one in to be "straightened out." Others call in order to come alone to prepare the therapist for his designated role. A subtype of this class comes prepared with a legal brief against the mate yet to be seen.

Some mates want to come alone at first because there is a "secret" which must be kept during the marital therapy, others because they want to form a coalition with the therapist against the other mate. Others think in terms of working on "the marriage" and want to come together from the first hour. A frequently encountered question is "Should we come separately or together?" By replying, "Which way would you prefer?", information gathering about the type of marriage and type of individuals involved within the marriage has begun.

Psychoanalytic Type of Initial Diagnostic Interview

In practice any outline of the initial diagnostic interview is utilized more as a general guide than as a routine procedure. The procedure is varied and modified as dictated by the input of information by the mate or mates. History taking when both mates are present usually necessitates greater activity and direction by the interviewer than when only one patient is present. This is to keep both mates involved in the interview and not have domination by one mate and a withdrawal by the other. Even as one mate is giving history, questions such as "Did you know that?" or "How do you feel about that?" involve the other mate and help clarify the relationship. The first interview may be conjoint, to be followed by individual interviews or vice versa. Patterns are sometimes determined by personal preference of the therapist or may be determined at the request of the mates. Each approach has advantages and disadvantages.

In marital therapy the diagnostic interview seeks to effect a dynamic understanding of each mate, and each person's contribution to the marital problem in order to determine what needs correction and which technique is most likely to achieve the desired result. Equally important is a determination as to whether either mate is committed to a personal change or to changing the mate.

A. Anamnestic Data

1. *Opening Presentation.* What are the chief complaints of each mate about the marriage, about each person, the children (nuclear family) and relatives (extended family)? Similarly, what are the positive factors in each of these areas? What needs reinforcement and what needs change? Even as effort is being made to recognize psychopathology, a therapeutic recognition and appreciation of strengths in the marriages is an important part of the history taking. The positive forces which can be marshaled for individual growth and development are as thoughtfully explored as destructive forces needing alteration. The positive forces that brought the two together originally and the dovetailing of needs that made the marriage operate originally are investigated, as well as the forces causing disturbance in the relationship.

In extremely pathological marriages, the bond that keeps the marriage together is a bond of hatred. It appears to us a paradox that a destructive force can be a bond. But the marital therapist must be aware that the beginning of the history taking is the beginning of a change orientation and that change of the bond of hatred by one of the mates which results in separation or divorce may remove the defense which has kept one mate emotionally intact. Loss of the relationship may result in regression with responses of panic and depression in the mate who appeared healthier while being maintained by the feelings of strength generated by hatred.

So we start with diagnosis not only of what has to be changed but also of what is available (if anything) to replace that which will be removed by the forthcoming changes. Marital therapy is more complicated than individual therapy since what may be beneficial for one mate may be disastrous for the other.

Psychotherapy of marital disharmony follows from the diagnosis of areas of incompatibility with an attempt to rectify them by one or more of the many techniques to be described in the following chapters. Rectifying them may lead to a strengthening of the relationship, the formation of a new and better relationship, or the loss of the relationship. Awareness of these possibilities accompanies the history taking, contributes to the diagnosis, determines the desirability or undesirability of treatment, and contributes to the selection of the type of treatment.

A current history, followed by a longitudinal history, of the marriage may be the starting point of the interview, during which time material on the character of each mate is collected. This is followed by a history of each individual (prior to their first meeting) to fill in the picture. Although the sequence is dictated by the needs of the mates, I prefer, soon after the chief complaints and current life and emotional involvements in the marriage, to begin with the life history of each individual prior to the beginning of their relationship. In this way, a psychodynamic understanding of each individual is available that makes the material about the beginning and the development of the relationship which led to marriage easier to understand. In brief, I try to understand: (1) who is this person who entered into this type of relationship with this specific other person, (2) how did this relationship promote, impede, or prevent the continuing growth and development of the individual, (3) what areas need correction, and (4) what is the best method of accomplishing this.

2. *Individual History of Each Mate.* After the opening material is presented, the life story of each individual is obtained in sequential fashion. This is not followed rigidly; shifting from past to present by the patient is frequently encountered. However, the patient is tactfully brought back to the longitudinal history at appropriate moments during the interview. Much of what follows is a modification of an outline originally published by Leon Saul (Saul, 1957).

Earliest memories. It is often helpful to start with the individuals' earliest memories. This serves many purposes. It takes some pressure off the marital disharmony by indicating an interest in the person other than in the marriage relationship. Although some earliest memories are pathognomonic of the character disorder and give an early insight into its contribution to the marital disorder, it is usually most helpful as another piece of evidence which, joined with what follows, clarifies the central emotional forces which need correction. The earliest memory leads to questions that are a means of finding out the images which the individual held of himself and of important family figures present in the memory or conspicuous by their absence. Also, the emotion accompanying the memory is very important.

The following is an unusually clear example of the matching of earliest memories that was helpful in understanding both the individual and interpersonal problems in their marriage. The wife's earliest memory was of insisting on sleeping on a cot in the dining room so she could listen to the family conversations in the parlor. When she could not tolerate her loneliness any longer, she would cry out and bring her father to her side. She then demanded that he carry her tenderly upstairs.

The husband's earliest memory was of having to take care of his retarded younger brother and not being able to do what he wanted to do with his peer group.

The psychotherapy followed this lead. She identified herself with a demanding, anxious child and demanded that her husband treat her as her father had. The husband identified her as his retarded brother whose constraint of his freedom caused resentment and emotional withdrawal.

First part of continuous memory. With the earliest memories as the starting point, the usual movement through knowledge about any childhood difficulties with feeding, toilet training, thumb sucking, bed wetting, childhood illnesses, phobias, or compulsions gives a picture of the individual prior to entering school. The history of the parents' marriage is important to understand identifications and repetitions in the patients' marriage. Family history is especially important where there is a possible primary affective disorder in a marriage partner.

History about school uncovers school phobias, scholastic adequacy, athletic abilities, and peer group relations that fill in the picture of the individual outside the family. This history through high school is extremely helpful together with the added aspects of masturbation, menarche, dating, and sexual experiences prior to the couple meeting.

It sets the stage for better understanding the history of the interpersonal relationship under scrutiny.

Dreams. While taking the first part of the continuous memory, a question about dreams fills in an understanding of that stage of growth and development. Recurrent dreams, in childhood and later, are an added contribution to the understanding of the central dynamic structure of the problem. Common types of dreams currently and throughout life fill in one more piece of the jigsaw puzzle being completed. Current dreams are likely to bring light to the marital problem. Some are unbelievably clarifying. (Example: Man with depression and onset of obsessive thoughts of suicide has a current dream of wife and two children who have fallen overboard from their sailboat. He is frantically but unsuccessfully trying to reach them before they drown. History that symptoms developed two months before, with marriage four months before to a widow with two children). Dreams of the night preceding the interview are likely to illustrate the marriage problem as above but also to refer to the interview and give important insight into the pre-meeting transference.

Fantasies. Conscious fantasies and daydreams about the marriage or marriage partner are asked for, as well as past, present, and long-continued fantasies.

Patients' fantasies are especially sensitive areas and many people tend to guard their daydreams, secret erotogenic stories, and mental images more carefully than information about overt behavior (Lowry and Lowry, 1975). A history that neglects fantasy is incomplete. The likelihood is that the stronger the defense against its exposure, the more important the fantasy life will be to the understanding of the central problem. To be tactful the examiner need not inquire into every detail but he must get the nature of the relationship between the participants in the fantasy. This is particularly enlightening to the sexual history.

Medical history. A good medical history is necessary for an evaluation of the person and for a sound diagnostic formulation. The close relationship between psyche and soma is particularly prominent with some patients (Martin, 1957). Differentiation is necessary between psychic problems which lead to somatic symptoms and organic conditions which cause psychological symptoms.

3. *History of the Marital Relationship.* With the individual histories up to the start of the relationship between the couples as a backdrop, the history of the interpersonal relationship is easier to understand. The reasons for the choice of the mate are investigated, as well as the marriage contract. The stages of the marriage are studied as related to the onset and course of complaints and symptoms of disharmony. Included in this section are the sexual history and considerations regarding the therapeutic contract.

The marriage contract. In the preceding chapter on the marriage contract, distinctions were made between the conscious spoken contract, the conscious unspoken contract, and the unconscious contract. The mates' material up to this point in the interview will already have revealed many of the unconscious aspects of the marriage contract. Further questioning about the contract will clarify conscious areas of agreement and disagreement and also allow for the therapist to reconstruct the unconscious areas of agreement and disagreement.

It might be well to mention at this point that as the therapist is evaluating the marriage contract each mate was capable of making and keeping with the other mate, he begins to evaluate the type of therapeutic contract each mate is likely to make with the therapist. This will be discussed later in this chapter.

It should be mentioned that in exploring the area of the marriage contract there is the entity of the absence of a conscious contract. There are marriages that take place without any discussion of individual or mutual expectations. The discovery of the absence of a contract leads to an important understanding of both the type of individuals involved in the relationship and the development of the marital disharmony. The lesser the conscious contract is present in the pre- or postmarriage contract, the greater is the influence of unconscious contract factors and influences from parental marriages.

The questioning in this area will follow from the leads given by the mates and is limited, as in other areas of initial diagnostic interviews, by the time available. In general, the following few questions contribute to the understanding that has been developing through the interview:

a) What qualities or characteristics of a mate were most important to you and why?

b) Are they still so important to you?

c) Are there others which have become important to you since your marriage?

d) What aspects of your life experiences influenced your preferences of attributes of a mate, and have your life experiences since then altered your preferences?

e) Did the preferences or expectations seem reasonable to you both before marriage? Do they seem reasonable to you now?

f) Do you want to change any values, attitudes, or feelings concerning your expectations of qualities in your mate? Do you want to change your mate's expectations of you? Do you want to change any of your mate's expectations for himself or herself?

Responses to such questions not only contribute to the diagnosis of the marital disharmony but also give a direction for the therapy which follows.

Sexual history. Many aspects of the sexual history will already have been uncovered without intensive questioning in this area. However, the sexual area is one most likely to be avoided or the facts of it disguised by most couples. This is also true for many interviewers, who need to overcome their own attitudes in this area in order to utilize interviewing as a means of evaluating the patients' sexual functions and attitudes and how they contribute to marital disharmony.

Chapter 3, on derivation of normal values in the sexual aspects of marriage, illustrated clinical material elicited from diagnostic interviewing in the areas of intercourse, physical intimacy, and emotional intimacy. Reference to this earlier chapter will contribute to history taking for the "normal" value system of diagnosis which follows.

The marital therapist should become very proficient in taking a sexual history. Sometimes sexual problems mask underlying individual and marital problems. The sexual history is important in detecting and understanding these problems, in order to determine whether they have to be rectified before a change in the sexual problems can take place, or whether a focus primarily upon the sexual problems (sex therapy) will be successful and will contribute to an alleviation of the individual or marital problems.

I will not go into great detail in this area because volumes on assessment of sexual function are now available. The Group for the Advancement of Psychiatry manual on *Assessment of Sexual Function* (1973) is excellent as a guide to interviewing, with detailed outlines for questioning and evaluation of sexual performance. It also contains an excellent list for further reading in this area.

It is of course important, as noted above, to take a good medical history to investigate physical causes of sexual dysfunction (Kaplan, 1974). In all sexual history taking, it is necessary to be sure that the material is not clouded by the presence of sexual dysfunction resulting from drug side effects. Story has published an extensive listing of such drugs and their effects (Story, 1974).

The three most important elements in taking a sexual history are that the therapist should (1) be comfortable in working in this area, (2) know what he is looking for, and (3) be innovative and meticulous in his questions to uncover the facts. If the therapist does not uncover the real problem, he does not know what treatment to prescribe or treats the disguise of the problem. However, the ethical considerations in sex therapy are present in the sexual history taking (Lowry and Lowry, 1975). As therapists become more comfortable in this area and more skillful in history taking, they are able to ask the necessary questions with understanding and objectivity. The questions, while yielding tactically useful information, also help to establish the examiner as trustworthy and knowledgeable.

The marital life cycle. As stated in a recent article by Berman and Lief (Berman and Lief, 1975), individual and marital development are inexorably entwined. The earlier chapters of this book on deriving normal values for marriage were based on Erikson's theories of psychosocial development (Erikson, 1968). Berman and Lief attempt to relate the marital life cycle to individual developmental tasks and stages as set forth by recent work on adult development that has been built on Erikson's theories. History taking from such a vantage point gives a broader perspective to the complicated and emotionally embedded material emanating from marital disharmony. Berman and Lief sharpen the awareness that it is crucial to recognize the critical stages in the individual life cycle. During history taking the marital therapist must be aware that issues that appear to be either purely individual or purely interpersonal are often the result of a complicated interaction between marital and individual crisis points.

History taking of the marital stages of development is directed to seeing if the marital task for that stage of development had been effected successfully, or what marital conflicts had developed. Berman and Lief divide the marital cycle into seven stages according to age groups:

Stage 1 (18-21 years). The marital task is to shift from family of origin to new commitment; the marital conflict is that original family ties conflict with adaptation.

Stage 2 (22-28 years). The task is provisional marital commitment; the conflict is uncertainty about choice of marital partner and stress over parenthood.

Stage 3 (29-31 years). The task is commitment crisis and dealing with restlessness; the conflict: doubts about choice come into sharp focus; rates of growth may diverge if spouse has not successfully negotiated stage 2 because of obligations as a parent.

Stage 4 (32-39 years). Marital task is productivity: children, work, friends and marriages; conflict is that husband and wife have different and conflicting ways of achieving productivity.

Stage 5 (40-42 years). Task is summing up; success and failure are evaluated and future goals sought; conflict is that husband and wife perceive "success" differently, with conflict between individual success and remaining in the marriage.

Stage 6 (43-59). Task is resolving conflicts and stabilizing the marriage for the long haul; conflict is conflicting rates and directions of emotional growth; concerns about losing youthfulness may lead to depression and/or acting out.

Stage 7 (60 years and over). Task is supporting and enhancing each other's struggle for productivity and fulfillment in the face of the threats of aging.

Although the above presentation was primarily drawn to describe people who marry in their twenties, it describes to some extent the stages that all married people go through.

The therapeutic contract. Working with marital partners and their marriage contracts offers an opportunity for insights into the establishment of a viable therapeutic contract that is not as easily recognized or reached in individual therapy. I have not seen this focus reported elsewhere in the literature and will begin the presentation of my investigations at this point because the process starts during the initial diagnostic interviews. Establishing, working, and reworking of the therapeutic contract does not take place until after the diagnostic interview and after a decision for treatment and time of treatment has been established.

We have seen that the marriage contract has a conscious (spoken and unspoken) part and an unconscious portion. Observations have shown that patients tend to make the same type of contract within the intimate therapeutic relationship as they make in the marital relationship. I will use the case material presented in the chapter on the marriage contract to illustrate the phenomenon.

In that example, it was observed that the partners each made a dishonest conscious contract with the other. She manipulated him into the marriage as a solution to her problems with a plan to change him after the marriage. He entered into the marriage so she would solve his social inadequacies while he pursued his goal of accumulation of wealth whose amount he would keep secret from her. Her unconscious contract was that she would be loved for herself, like a baby, no matter what she did and that her unceasing demands would never be resented. His unconscious contract was that he would be appreciated for what he chose to give and would be left alone to do what he wanted to do.

It seems clear that the contracts involved transference reactions. Her identification was as an irresponsible child and her transference was to a good mother—the role she expected her husband to fulfill. The husband's identification was with his long-suffering father. His father had devoted his life to his business and to be doing what he wanted to do even if he had to lie and deny his wife's hurt feelings and bitter tirades against him. The patient saw his wife as the cold, unloving, critical mother he had experienced in his childhood. The fixed identifications and fixed transferences determined the rigidity of the unworkable marriage contract.

In the therapeutic situation, prior to my intervention, each established a therapeutic contract analogous to the marital contract. The wife consciously withheld information that would illustrate her problems. She was not in treatment to change herself but to seduce me into agreeing that she was "right" and thus to gain an ally in her unrelenting effort to change her husband into what she needed him to be. Her unconscious contract involved her fixed transefrence measures. It was the one described above with her husband, a child-good mother relationship. In this she expected the therapist to fall in love with her and marry her and be the husband that her husband could not be.

The husband also was consciously dishonest in the therapeutic situation. He withheld information, told lies that were only exposed in the conjoint sessions, and strove to continue to do what he wanted to do, while pretending otherwise, to keep his wife from losing control. His initial transference to me was the mother transference, but once he realized that I was not taking sides, an underlying father transference took place. In this, he saw me as an ally who would understand his business dealings and who would show him how to achieve his financial goals. It does sometimes follow that, through a new understanding of interpersonal relations, such individuals become more successful in their businesses, and the therapy to them is a business venture through which they experience a high return on their financial investment. This becomes a source of resistance to changing their personality structures to resolve the marital impasse.

Knowledge of the marital contract and of the conscious and unconscious therapeutic contract allows for interpretation of noneffective contracts and a rewriting of workable therapeutic contracts. It is not uncommon in the type of referrals described in the introductory chapter to find that no workable therapeutic contract had been established. It is the observation that many people go "for" treatment but are not "in" treatment. Early clarification of a workable therapeutic contract and repeated clarifications throughout treatment are extremely helpful to patients who often are confused in treatment and do not know what is expected of them in treatment, let alone agree or disagree with it.

If the therapist continuously clarifies the therapeutic contract and is successful in establishing a working contract with the marital couple, it becomes an excellent model for the partners to follow in establishing a workable marriage contract.

It is also important to emphasize that the therapeutic contract involves a conscious and unconscious aspect for the therapist. It is expected that the conscious contract of the therapist will be an honest one, although this is not always so. The unconscious contract of the therapist involves his countertransference reactions. In an early paper on countertransference in treatment of marriage partners, we stated that the countertransference was the most important factor in the treatment of marriage problems (Bird and Martin, 1956). Although we have since changed from this viewpoint, there is no doubt about the importance of countertransference in psychotherapy of marital partners.

In this part of the diagnostic interview unconscious associative material is listened to for understanding of the transference and countertransference phenomena. Just as described above, we use the marriage contract material to understand the transference, we listen to the interview data for indications of how the transference will develop and of the patients' attitudes, conscious and unconscious, toward the therapist. These clues help to understand the patients' current motivation.

The countertransference is used as a guide in understanding the patients. The therapist can sense within himself feelings which are unusually strong. This reaction is used as a clue to the motivations in the patient that evoke them. In addition, when treating marital partners, the therapist's reactions to one patient can help him understand a similar reaction by the mate to this evoking characteristic.

Diagnosis

The initial diagnostic interviews may necessitate several sessions, including individual and conjoint sessions. During these sessions the therapist is formulating his diagnoses. Diagnoses may be made (1) by personality style and psychiatric terminology of each mate, (2) by types of marriages as presented in Chapter 2, or (3) by the following diagnostic schema which evolved from the earlier derivation of normal values for marriage.

"NORMAL" VALUE SYSTEM OF DIAGNOSIS
OF MARITAL DISHARMONY

The following capacities are evaluated by the interviewer during initial interviews, leading to formulation of tentative diagnosis and plan of therapy.

Each Partner Individually

1. Capacity for independence (to stand alone)
2. Capacity for supportiveness to mate
3. Capacity to accept support from mate
4. Capacity for lust (intercourse)
5. Capacity for sensuousness (physical intimacy)
6. Capacity for love (emotional intimacy)

The Marriage Contract

1. Conscious Contract

   a. Areas of agreement
   b. Areas of disagreement

2. Unconscious Contract

   a. Areas of agreement
   b. Areas of disagreement

Diagnosis follows from the type of initial diagnostic interview conducted by the examiner and is based on the therapist's theoretical constructs. Obviously, there will be wide variations in emphasis during interviews and in formulations. Given competent therapists, however, the essential picture, though described with different terminology, should be the same.

AN ILLUSTRATION OF A PSYCHOANALYTIC TYPE OF CONJOINT MARITAL EVALUATION

The following initial diagnostic interview illustrates the preceding outline. It is a combination of interviews and a changing of facts for the protection of the couples involved. However, the marital pattern and the interview technique are typical ones. The notes which indicate observations of the interviewer are intended to help the reader become aware of the nonverbal communication to which the interviewer was responding and which was not transmitted through the printed communication.

Dr. Martin: Tell me about the marital problem that brings you here.

Jack: Would you care to begin?

Jane: Go ahead, Jack. [Jane is being cautious. She sets Jack up until she decides the safest approach.]

Jack: The whole problem was precipitated by her leaving me, but I think the roots go deeper than that and that we've got some conflicts as to what the aims and the goals of our marriage ought to be and the way we go about achieving them. We've got ideas about what the other person should be, what role they should play, and things don't seem to be coming out as planned, at least that's the way it appears. [Jack is the logical thinker in the marriage.]

Dr. Martin: Could you elaborate on that?

Jack: Well, we'll each have to elaborate for each other, but, well, it seems that I'm not coming up to Jane's expectations as a husband, as a breadwinner—and as a lover, as well, I guess— and this has caused her to become alienated. From my point of view, there is a dependency on this; I expect a great deal of loyalty from my spouse and this has been undercut as well. It depends upon my failings. It's very complex. [The theme of unfulfilled expectations is identified early.]

Dr. Martin: Jane, how do you feel about this?

Jane: Well, I think this is the first time I've heard Jack describe our early problems like that and it's what I feel and it's what we talk about sometimes. Mostly on my part, I'm really emotionally immature and use people and opportunities outside our marriage to try and help me make up for all my failings in our marriage and for what I consider Jack's failings, but, he said it better than I did cause I . . . [Jane's difficulty in thinking clearly and ending up confused and silent is noted.]

Dr. Martin: What do you consider Jack's failings?

Jane: Well, they're really dumb things to consider: his ability to make money, to provide for me as a wife. I didn't want to compete. I felt that if I'm going to be earning money and working all the time, that I might as well be single, you know, and I didn't really care about being married all that much as long as it was going to be a fifty-fifty sort of roommate, buddy sort of situation, instead of a loving husband and wife, and the more it seemed that I had to play that kind of a role the less I wanted to be married, so I just didn't consider myself very married, and I left. [Jane's expectation of financial security was unfulfilled. The marriage contract as she had consciously wanted but not expressed it was being broken. The unconscious contract was that she would be taken care of as a child ("Loving husband and wife"—a "love-sick" wife talking).]

[Silence.]

Dr. Martin: How long have you been married? [The beginning of the marital history.]

Jack: We've been married two and a half years.

Dr. Martin: When did your problems begin?

Jack: Well . . .

Jane: Immediately. I left him after three months.

Dr. Martin: What brought you together again.

Jane: My hospitalization.

Dr. Martin: Tell me about that.

Jane: It seems that I couldn't handle my job and other relationships and I had a type of reaction where I wasn't quite sure what I was doing. I wasn't able to do anything and I ended up in the hospital. I started thinking about what I really wanted and I decided that I really wanted the security of my husband. [Further material about her difficulty in thinking and clear material about limited capacity for independence.]

Dr. Martin: What were your symptoms that led to your being in the hospital?

Jane: I really don't know, my husband brought me in.

Dr. Martin: What do you remember about it?

Jane: Uh, I was, I don't remember much about it. I guess I was incoherent. I tried to tell Jack the other day what it was like; it wasn't a religious experience, but it was just that I couldn't cope with what was going on, so I just sort of withdrew into myself to the point that externally I was just, I was confused.

Dr. Martin (*to Jack*): What did you observe?

Jack: Well, she was completely incoherent, she would talk on and on in broken fragments, which seemed to have inner consistency to her. She was very nervous, you know, looked about very nervously, glancing around all the time and generally did not seem to be too much in contact with her environment. Like I could say something and it would not register.

Dr. Martin: Jane, how long were you in the hospital? [Therapist's decision to establish relationship by use of the first name.]

Jane: I think about three and a half weeks.

Dr. Martin: How long is it since you've been out?

Jane: Two weeks.

Dr. Martin: Good, all right, so we start fresh now to help you. [Continued effort to establish therapeutic relationship and beginning effort to spell out therapeutic contract.]

Jane: Yes.

Dr. Martin: Tell me something about your early history, where you were born, what sort of family you came from, your picture of yourself as a child. [Beginning of individual history following early description of the marital problem.]

Jane: I was born in Chicago and as a child I was, I guess I was a happy child, and I liked to read. I can remember as a child that my activities were more centered around a good book than anything else. [Possible reference to lack of or avoidance of relationship with mother and father.]

Dr. Martin: What is your earliest memory in life?

Jane: I don't know. [Frequent response, since many individuals have never thought about it.]

Dr. Martin: Take your time, what is the first thing you remember? Reading a book?

Jane: Well, uh, I have a sense of what I was like as a small child from what my parents have told me. Of certain activities that were going on, I guess going to my grandmother's house is what I can really remember; the excitement of getting up early and going on a trip to my grandmother's house. My grandmother was, we stayed with her in the summer, that's where I learned to swim and do all the things that weren't attached to school, and I got away from my parents that way too. [Further information of early difficulty in relation to parents and importance of grandmother as a source of pleasure.]

Dr. Martin: Who's we?

Jane: My brother and myself.

Dr. Martin: Is he older or younger?

Jane: My brother's older than I am.

Dr. Martin: How much older?

Jane: He's four years older than I am, he's thirty.

Dr. Martin: All right, and these early memories of your grand-mother's place—how old were you at that time?

Jane: Well, I went there, I was taken there when I was about two or three weeks old, but I can remember being, oh, six or seven and going on a train by myself with my brother there. [Early separation from mother. Grandmother a mother substitute.]

Dr. Martin: Where was this?

Jane: In Iowa.

Dr. Martin: And what did you enjoy the most while you were there?

Jane: No spankings and a lot of cookies.

Dr. Martin: Your grandparents loved you?

Jane: Very much.

Dr. Martin: And you reciprocated.

Jane: Yes.

Dr. Martin: And what was the picture of you and your brother, how did the two of you get along?

Jane: When we were younger we got along very well, but then we went through all the stages that brothers and sisters go through.

Dr. Martin: When did that begin?

Jane: Right after puberty for both of us.

Dr. Martin: All right, so the early days on the farm were pleasant days? [Wanting to fill in earlier picture.]

Jane: They were.

Dr. Martin: Now tell me your earliest memory of your mother. The picture of what she was like physically, how she re-sponded to you.

Jane: I have real guilt feelings about my mother so anything I would say would be things that have happened in the last five years, and they have made me change my opinion about her.

Dr. Martin: Well, first try to remember your earliest images of your mother.

Jane: I guess I see her with my father before I was born. As a child I can't, I don't see, I can't think of any other way than what I see in pictures of her. [A confusing response; her difficulty in understanding my question?]

Dr. Martin: What do you mean when you say before you were born?

Jane: Well, I can, as a child, okay, I can see myself looking at pictures in an album before I was born, during the war, standing by the car or something.

Dr. Martin: What did they look like in the pictures?

Jane: They looked like two handsome young people.

Dr. Martin: Can you describe your mother's coloring. [Probing for nature of relationship with mother.]

Jane: She has black hair and she has dark eyes and she is, she's small and has very nice legs, and apparently when my parents were first married, they were in love with each other, so she was happy then I suppose.

Dr. Martin: Until when?

Jane: Hum?

Dr. Martin: You say when they were first married.

Jane: Oh. They were always fighting. But, they stayed together all those years because they had three kids and my father doesn't believe in divorce and I guess my mother did more. [Favors her father.]

Dr. Martin: What age is the third child?

Jane: Sixteen.

Dr. Martin: All right, now what sort of personality did your mother have when you were a child? [Still trying to clarify the mother-child relationship.]

Jane: My mother came from a farm near a small town, and she was bedazzled by the city life, and she enjoyed it. She wanted to get away from the farm life, and she got off on the wrong track, she lost all her values for life, for humanity, for human beings by having to—I don't know, this is the way I feel—by being in the city. She just forgot how to love people I guess.

Dr. Martin: Did you feel that your mother didn't love you when you were a child?

Jane: She didn't love my father and she took it out on us kids.

Dr. Martin: Did you love her?

Jane: Up until a couple of years ago when I figured out what she was doing to me, yeah.

Dr. Martin: And what was your father like as a person?

Jane: He was a very considerate, kind, warm, understanding person. I love my father very much.

Dr. Martin: What sort of work does he do?

Jane: He's an accountant.

Dr. Martin: And what sort of a student were you in school?

Jane: I was a good student up until I started having problems with my health, my mental health, emotionally.

Dr. Martin: What age was that?

Jane: Oh, that was about twenty.

Dr. Martin: What were you like in the early elementary grades, do you have any picture of yourself? [An attempt to develop a chronological sequence of events.]

Jane: I was okay, I was just a regular kid.

Dr. Martin: Did you get along with the other children?

Jane: Um, yes, I guess so, yes. I tend to remember, I'm so pessimistic. I tend to remember all the negative, sometimes negative things. [Peer group relations questionable. An attempt to avoid recognition of difficulty in this area.)

Dr. Martin: Like what? What do you remember?

Jane: Oh, I don't know. The feelings of loneliness that I think children have.

Dr. Martin: What high school did you go to? [Feeling tone of elementary school recognized, an attempt to move interview along.]

Jane: A Chicago public high school.

Dr. Martin: And what sort of student were you there?

Jane: I was a stormy student. I would sometimes get all really good high grades and then sometimes I wouldn't. But I came out with a pretty good average. I was a good student. I was pretty good. [Again illustrating her difficulty in thinking clearly.]

Dr. Martin: What was your honor point average?

Jane: Oh, three point something. B's and A's, whatever that is.

Dr. Martin: How old were you when you started to menstruate? [Important to history of puberty and adolescence.]

Jane: Thirteen, probably.

Dr. Martin: And do you remember that?

Jane: Uh, no I don't, because that's what everybody was doing at that time.

Dr. Martin: So you don't remember how you took it; did you take it well, as a matter of course?

Jane: Yeah, I think that the school system that I was in had us pretty well educated to accept things like that, more so than from the family type point of view. The school, the girl scouts, the school and everything.

Dr. Martin: And how old were you when you started dating?

Jane: Fifteen.

Dr. Martin: And how did it go with dating?

Jane: It went all right. [Evasiveness.]

Dr. Martin: Did you have enough dates?

Jane: I didn't think so at the time. Not with the people that I wanted to. [Premarital difficulties clear from childhood and thereafter.]

Dr. Martin: Were you in love in high school?

Jane: Yeah.

Dr. Martin: One particular boy? More than one?

Jane: I guess he was a father substitute more than anything else. Of course, I had been sort of ostracized from the high school situation by a fellow who cut off all my connections with the high school peer group, and I started dating someone, I think he was twenty-one and he was out of school of course, and I started hanging around with a group of girls who were outside the high school situation. So, it wasn't like I had a date for the football game. [Again in difficulty with peer group and reluctant to take the responsibility upon herself.]

Dr. Martin: Did you go on to college? [Pushing the longitudinal history along.]

Jane: Yes, I did.

Dr. Martin: Tell me about that.

Jane: I was really happy to get away, because I could start all over again and I met some really wonderful people.

Dr. Martin: Where?

Jane: At the University of Illinois, and I went through school.

Dr. Martin: Graduated there?

Jane: Yes.

Dr. Martin: And what was your honor point in college?

Jane: Pretty low, well, the last, it was a B average almost all the way through, until my parents starting getting their divorce and then they started kicking me out of the house every time I came home and doing stuff like that, things that upset me; I didn't realize that I was upset about that as much as I was. I should have sought help then, but I didn't and my grades went right down. I don't know. I didn't do so well as I had.

Dr. Martin: Did you date a lot?

Jane: Yes. I had plenty of people to go out with.

Dr. Martin: What religion are you? [Filling in the pieces of the history.]

Jane: Me? I'm not any religion.

Dr. Martin: In what religion were you raised?

Jane: Protestant, but I went over to being a Catholic when I was dating a fellow in college.

Dr. Martin: Can we move on to your history of sexual relationships?

Jane: Do I have to talk about that now?

Dr. Martin: No, we can wait until we meet alone next time, if you wish. Can you tell me about your first meeting with Jack?

Jane: It was really nice. I met him at a party, and I, we fell in love. I really felt that I loved him when I first met him, and I was really happy, I was really thankful that someone finally married me. I felt like, like I wanted to be married and that's all. [Did she get married because she loved him or because she wanted to be married and he was the only one who would marry her?]

Dr. Martin: And how long did you go together before you got married?

Jack: Four months, five months.

Jane: Two months.

Jack: No, four months.

Jane: Four months?

Jack: Um-huh.

Jane: Okay, oh yeah, you're right honey. [Illustrating her need to please him at this time.]

Dr. Martin: And did you have sexual relations before marriage.

Jane: Yes.

Dr. Martin: Were they satisfying?

Jane: Yeah, I guess so. (Turning to look at Jack.)

Jack: Speak for yourself.

Jane: Yes they were, I didn't know any better. [Meaning that they weren't.]

Dr. Martin: And what did you find out when you knew better?

Jane: Oh, that was a leading thing for me to say. I don't really know, because right now I don't have any feelings whatsoever about sex; it's kind of the whole subject that got me into trouble and they were really torrid, sordid experiences that I had. Now I have to go back and settle my values and change my personality so that I don't run into this problem again. [Reference to experiences between Jane's leaving Jack and calling for him to rescue her at the hospital.]

Dr. Martin: Could you help me understand, resettle your values from what to what?

Jane: From what I feel sex is. I don't know, from not considering my marriage as anything special and to considering that a marriage is something to work at and that the rest will all fall in, I mean, in due time, it will happen. [Is she saying to give up torrid sex for security of marriage with Jack? And in due time sex will work out?]

Dr. Martin: Jack, could you help me by telling me about your-self? What is your earliest memory in life? [Switch to diag-nostic interview of Jack's premarital life.]

Jack: My earliest memory is riding the diesel electric to go Christmas shopping.

Dr. Martin: What age?

Jack: Two and a half.

Dr. Martin: And with whom?

Jack: My parents and I guess an uncle or an aunt or two.

Dr. Martin: And is that a very happy memory?

Jack: Oh yes, I think that I was surprised to hear that Jane's earliest memory was of trains, so I guess that trains must impress children a lot cause they are so big and powerful. [He misses that the importance of Jane's earliest memory was not trains but going from an unhappy home to Grand-mother's.]

Dr. Martin: What is your memory of what your mother and father looked like at that age and what sort of people they were.

Jack: Oh, they were middle class people and they loved each other very much and still do. They were just the greatest thing in the world as far as I'm concerned.

Dr. Martin: Describe them physically for me.

Jack: My father is short and heavy; he's, they are both older people, they didn't have children until they were well on, so I never knew them otherwise than middle aged people as I got to be a little older, so they just seemed to have a great deal of love for each other; you know, pride and integrity and any other values you'd care to give a child.

Dr. Martin: And how did they treat you?

Jack: Fairly well. [?]

Dr. Martin: Both the same?

Jack: Both the same, they both, I have an older brother also, no younger brother, and they both loved us a great deal, and there wasn't too much sibling rivalry by the way, and I remember getting a whacking when I clearly deserved it; punishment was something that was reserved for something that was really a defined and specific provocation. [His denial of sibling rivalry an affirmation? Minimizing the punishment he received and its effect upon him?]

Dr. Martin: In your earliest memory is your brother with the family on the train?

Jack: I guess he'd have to be, but mainly I remember the train.

[His strong involvement with the importance of power.]

Dr. Martin: And what is the picture you have of yourself as a child?

Jack: Well, a lot of the time I think I was by myself. I liked to be by myself a lot and this seldom shaded over into loneliness because I had friends when I wanted them, so I read a lot as a child, like Jane, and collected things and did a lot of just activities. [Frequent use of mechanism of denial (here loneliness).]

Dr. Martin: How were you different from your brother?

Jack: Well, in the sixth grade, I was sent to, I wasn't performing in school and I went to a Catholic school and I wasn't doing well there, so my parents heard about a special school and they sent me off for testing.

Dr. Martin: How did you test?

Jack: I tested well. It takes a 130 to get in. Anyway, I spent the next three years there, but it didn't even create any sibling rivalry, even though my brother, who was just entering high school at the time could have been, I guess, reasonably put out by my performance and the idea that I was being coddled and being sent off to special schools and what not, but we rode it out fairly well, I think. I wound up going to the same high school as him and he put me under his wing and kind of played the big brother act and that did it for him. [Apparent need to deny sibling rivalry.]

Dr. Martin: What was your honor point in high school?

Jack: Quite high, we did it on a percentage system. I would say it was about 95 percent.

Dr. Martin: How did you get along socially?

Jack: Fairly well.

Dr. Martin: Did you participate in sports?

Jack: No, not in high school.

Dr. Martin: Then you went on to Illinois?

Jack: Yes.

Dr. Martin: And tell me about your experiences there.

Jack: Well, I did not have the greatest preparation for going to a great big worldly multiversity, and I soon found all my kind of agnostic and rational tendencies that I had been developing in high school pretty well undercut. But, I did well and my grades were fine, I was in the honors program and I stayed in that for three years until I got married and did fairly well; socially, you know, so-so.

Dr. Martin: Have you had any recurring dreams throughout

your life, the same dream that would come back? [Filling in unconscious material.]

Jack: I had a dream. It was not a recurring dream, it was kind of a progression, it got very, very interesting as it went on. I used to keep having the dream earlier in college that I was being sent back to high school because I had not completed certain requirements and all of a sudden I would find myself back in the same classroom with these people I had gone to high school with, except they were the same age that they'd been in high school and I was older and I was just "sick unto death" for being there and couldn't understand why, and this continued for a long time, until about a year ago, and the shaping gradually took on different tones. I began to have the situation change so that I was back there, sometimes in a teaching capacity, but still it was the wrong place for me; or even before that, I felt that I had gone back and somehow placed out of it. You know, they'd say, we want you back here to check on it and that was that. But, gradually I began to cope with this dream within the context of the dream and after a while, well, I haven't had it lately. It seemed a very interesting way to cope with a recurring dream. [Indication of ego persistence, search for mastery and capacity to either resolve or repress problems?]

Dr. Martin: Do you remember any childhood dreams?

Jack: Nothing that stayed with me through the years. I imagine that there were some things that really seemed important at the time but nothing. . . .

Dr. Martin: Nightmares?

Jack: No.

Dr. Martin: Jane, do you remember any childhood dreams and recurrent dreams throughout the years? [To bring her back into the flow of material.]

Jane: There is only one dream that I can really remember. It's when I get up and have to go somewhere and get dressed. My sisters and I used to always share our clothes because we were all around the same size and I used to dream that I'd go to the closet to borrow my little sister's clothes to get ready for wherever I have to go. I just dreamed it last night. [Her identity problem?]

Dr. Martin: To borrow your little sister's clothes?

Jane: Yes, well she's just the same size as me, but she's younger.

Dr. Martin: Do you wear the same style of clothes? [Questioning her lack of sense of identity.]

Jane: Yeah, except that now I'm getting older and we don't exactly wear the same style of clothes anymore. She has a lot of clothes. She's a sharp dresser. It's sort of like I've had this personality change and I wish to change my personality to appear younger, I guess. [Would rather be her sister than herself?]

Dr. Martin: Do you remember any childhood nightmares?

Jane: No.

Dr. Martin: Jack, let's go back to you then. When did you start dating? [To complete his history.]

Jack: It's hard to say. There was a social life at high school. But, being from a suburban community and never having gone to school in a school system, your style is pretty cramped until you've got your driver's licence, so you know, there was socializing around the school, you know, sitting together in classes and things like that, but, if you mean going out at night type dating, the world is on wheels. [A lot of words with which to say no.]

Dr. Martin: Did you fall in love with anyone before you met Jane?

Jack: In retrospect, no. [A common response.]

Dr. Martin: No, I mean at the time.

Jack: No, I don't really think so. You just say you've got a crush on so and so or you'd really like to go out with so and so and things like that. Especially in retrospect I really can't tell.

Dr. Martin: You never had a love affair before you met Jane.

Jack: What is a love affair?

Dr. Martin: Very intimately involved, sexual relationships.

Jack: Yes.

Dr. Martin: You did. Then tell me about Jane; when you met her, how you felt about her. [A mental note made to pursue this in interview with him alone.]

Jack: Well, the first thing that struck me about her was that she had a lot of class. She was very aware and had a great deal of, what should I say, just a really aesthetic appreciation of life and a great deal of poetic sensibilitiy and everything. I just thought she was a really terrific person.

Dr. Martin: And you fell in love with her?

Jack: Yes.

Dr. Martin: This time you knew that you were in love?

Jack: Yes. I took the big step.

Dr. Martin: And married her.

Jack: Yes, besides I thought she was very sexy.

Jane: I was fat and you know it. [Depreciated self-image.]

Jack: You were not. She thinks that any person that doesn't belong in Dachau is fat. This is fat for her.

Dr. Martin: Is that how you feel about yourself now?

Jane: No, I don't feel that way now.

Jack: That's just because you woke up this morning and you weighed 104 instead of 105.

Jane: No, I don't think that's fat.

Dr. Martin: Do you have a thing about weight?

Jane: Yeah I do, because at one time I got very fat—about thirty pounds overweight. I was used to being slim and trim and I guess because I was upset or something, I ate a lot and I got up to about 130-135.

Dr. Martin: When was this?

Jane: This was when I was about twenty-one or twenty-two and then when I met Jack, I guess I wasn't fat, I was just a big girl. [Confusion in body image.]

Dr. Martin: What did you weigh when you met Jack?

Jane: I'm not saying.

Jack: Oh, we both know.

Jane: I weighed more than he did to tell the truth.

Jack: Well, that's not saying much, I weighed 128.

Jane: He weighed about 128, and I weighed about 130. Then I lost a lot of weight and got back to where I wanted to be.

Jack: And I started eating home cooking, as opposed to my own, so we've gone like that (gesturing with hands up and down).

Dr. Martin: What was there about Jack that made you fall in love with him?

Jane: I felt that he was a very understanding person, and he seemed to know how to treat me so that I could be myself instead of pretending that I didn't care. I don't know, it's a terrible thing to say, he told me some of the fantasies that had happened in his life and I understood completely what he was talking about.

Dr. Martin: What were they?

Jane: What were some of the fantasies?

Dr. Martin: What did he tell you?

Jane: What did he tell me? About being desperate sometimes, taking measures against himself. He was studying Zen Buddhism, I think, at the time, weren't you? [A piece of history that would not have come out if she had not brought it up.]

Jack: Yeah, I guess so, yeah.

Jane: And I had some interests in a philosophical sense. It just seemed that he could understand, I feel like I'm not speaking very well.

Dr. Martin: You're doing well. Just continue.

Jane: And I just felt that empathy was the way, I guess. That he had the same kind of understanding about the ways I felt. That's how I felt. [A communion of souls that turned out to be more fantasy than reality.]

Dr. Martin: Jack, you didn't tell me how desperate you had felt. Can you tell me about it? [One of the advantages of the conjoint interview.]

Jack: Desperate is not exactly the word. I would get into very deep depressions, sometime about my freshman and early sophomore year. I guess I wasn't adjusting really, really well. I felt that I wasn't moving into the crowd too well. Of course, you can go around campus for months at a time and not see any familiar face especially if you're a freshman, and I guess that this hit me hard and specifically what I used to do, you know, I'd feel really hostile, and I was also into a pain type of thing.

Dr. Martin: A pain type of thing?

Jack: I used to inflict pain on myself.

Dr. Martin: Doing what?

Jack: Razor blades, scalpels and things like that. I've always had a fascination with pain anyway, and I have a very high threshold of pain and sometimes with complete clinical dispassion I would sit there and test my pain threshold the same way a person would learn to walk over hot rocks. [Again the theme, as in dream sequence, of ego controls and mastery of one's sensations.]

Dr. Martin: Do you still do this?

Jack: No.

Dr. Martin: Did he tell you about this?

Jane: Yeah he did. I saw the scar on his arm and he told me about it. I was typing a paper for someone else and all of a sudden I sort of experienced what he must have been experiencing and that's why I said desperate measures, because that's the way it looked to me. When we were first married, he used to punish himself for things that I used to do, but now it's out of the question; it's something that I would never expect him to do again.

Dr. Martin: So that you have matured in this marriage?

Jack: Oh yes, but I saw a psychiatrist later on after this. I got

kind of shipped off to him. My parents discovered that I
had been taking drugs, nothing really outstanding, but to
them the word drugs . . . I mean they packed me off. . . .
[Denial of seriousness of problem?]

Dr. Martin: This was in your first and second years at college?

Jack: Yeah. This was after my freshman year, and in the summer
I let slip a few choice references and so. . . .

Dr. Martin: Like what?

Jack: Well, they were talking about the evils of marijuana and
I said, "What do you really know about marijuana first
hand," and they said, "Oh," you know, and they sent me
to a very good psychiatrist who took a completely different
approach and we talked; I didn't have very many sessions
with him actually. This was just during the summer and he
sent me off with a blessing after a fairly short time. By the
time I got to him, I felt secure enough that I could mention
these things to my parents. They were more or less in the
past or under control anyway, so I reinforced my own behavior sufficiently so that at the time what we did was reinforce it more through discussion and points.

Dr. Martin: When you worked with him were you still cutting
yourself?

Jack: No.

Dr. Martin: And when you worked with him you didn't have
any depression?

Jack: No.

Dr. Martin: Have you had any depression recently?

Jack: No.

Dr. Martin: Even with this upset with Jane? You haven't gotten
depressed?

Jack: No.

Dr. Martin: All right, and when you *did* have depression, how
low did you get?

Jack: Well, it seemed like the end of the world at the time. You
just . . . it's really hard to say. I just didn't know where I
stood, I was just a young punk kid who had gotten to the
University and really felt kind of rootless. That's how I
put it now.

Dr. Martin: And what's helped you to feel better?

Jack: I've gotten on much better terms with my environment.
I had a lot of experiences and all sorts of things since then,
and things that I come up against I've come up against at
least once before.

Dr. Martin: Jane, how does that sound to you? Is that the way you saw him when you married him?

Jane: Yeah. He'd been through a lot. Both of us have had to handle a lot of situations in the context of the marriage and out of it, in terms of work and things like that that have made us more responsible people. I'm sorry I brought that up, I didn't mean to.

Jack: No. If that qualifies me as having a "past psychiatric history," then actually it's very important.

Jane: Okay. [Still fearful of losing his protection.]

Dr. Martin: Everything has to come out here as we work together. [Therapeutic contract emphasis.]

Jack: There was something I was about to mention. This came up yesterday or the day before. There was another reason that she was attracted to me and I just found out about it.

Jane: (Laughing) What?

Jack: Because of my dynamite social life?

Jane: Oh yeah.

Jack: Yeah, because I partied a lot at the time. We met at a party, as she already said and since then we don't party at all. We've become two great stick-in-the-mud homebodies and we don't get out nearly as much as either of us would like to. But, our timing is very bad mutually. [Marriage contract—superficial values.]

Jane: What also attracted me to you was that you had a lot of money to spend. [Marriage contract—superficial values.]

Jack: Yeah. We met during the summer and I was working in a factory. I paid my way through school and, of course, a kid with a summer job in a factory is just rolling in dough because he's got no expenses, and I was living at home and everything, so it looked like I was Mr. Big Bucks. If you would put two and two together and realize that I was going to quit my job in two months. . . .

Jane: I know (laughing).

Dr. Martin: You seem to be able to laugh together. You seem close with one another. What went wrong in this marriage?

Jane: I think a lot of emotional problems. Things that I never let go of when I got married. People that I refused to let go, friendships.

Dr. Martin: Explain that to me, I don't understand.

Jane: When I got married, I didn't have a lot of self-confidence and Jack gave me the confidence to go out and teach and take care of a home and so when he built my confidence up and people—men—started looking at me, I just never reacted like I was married. [Her lack of gratitude illustrating tenuousness of her relationships.]

Dr. Martin: Why?

Jane: I guess . . . I don't know, that's why I'm here because I don't know why.

Dr. Martin: What's the first thought that comes to mind as to why you did that?

Jane: Because I always felt that the two years that I was sick were two years that were taken away from me. Two youth years that I never got to experience, because I was so emotionally upset all the time, and I didn't have a lot of friends because of that. I mean the friends I did have I still have and they are really good friends. I can call them up any time and have a conversation with them, but I just felt, I guess it was sort of like a revenge.

Dr. Martin: Did you have any psychiatric treatment?

Jane: I was hospitalized.

Dr. Martin: Where?

Jane: At a private hospital in Chicago. I don't know the name of it.

Dr. Martin: For two years?

Jane: No. For six weeks.

Jack: Twice.

Jane: Twice.

Dr. Martin: What did you learn from your work with your psychiatrist?

Jane: He never talked to me . . . he never even asked my name.

Dr. Martin: So there wasn't anything you learned from that experience?

Jane: No, except a lot of pain, a lot of fear of hospitals.

Jack: Perhaps you should mention your chief form of therapy.

Jane: Shock therapy.

Jack: Electric shock.

Jane: Electric shock.

Dr. Martin: Sounds like you had a real rough time for two years.

Jane: Well after trying to . . . well, my parents didn't know what a good psychiatrist was and they took me to this man who hospitalized me and gave me shock therapy and I therefore had a huge fear . . . I was afraid when it was happening, I was afraid afterwards and then my parents started kicking me out of the house all the time because they had so many problems. They deny it now, but they did when I came home. So, the second time I signed myself in and I was there for ... I had hair about down to here and I cut it all off this long and I felt that I was being self-destructive and I needed some protection, so I went back into the hospital a second time for another six weeks. This was in a two-year time period when all my friends were graduating and getting married and having a normal life and I felt that somewhere along the line I really slipped up and that I was being battered about. I feel that way now. I was supposed to do my student teaching, and I was living at home with my parents, and my mother was such a tyrant. But anyway, that was when I had the two hospitalizations, and Dr. X. has really helped me a lot being in the hospital this time. It's really helped me a lot, this type of treatment, and I wish I could have been sent here the first time, because I don't think I would ever have had to come back.

Dr. Martin: All right, good.

Jack: It was tough getting Jane to see a doctor in any capacity for a while there. This had taken a great toll on her confidence and the reaction was fairly strong.

Dr. Martin: Jane, if I understand you, you had these very bad two years and then you came out of it, you met Jack and you felt his love and interest in you. Something about the relationship helped you to come out of yourself and to do better, but you didn't stay there with him, but you went on making up for lost time or enjoying what you hadn't had before?

Jane: I think that's it.

Dr. Martin: And how did you feel about Jack when you were doing this?

Jane: At first I felt very guilty about it and I'd go to church and I'd go to confession and I'd cry and I was trying to get him to forgive me for what he didn't even know he was forgiving me for, and then when I started ... I don't know, it doesn't seem right now, the whole thing seems totally wrong for me to do. It just doesn't, when I think about it, just because I can't even remember the circumstances that made me so mad at him and I felt justified in going out with somebody else. I think we've gone over and over that incident that first started it when we were first married so much that. . . .

Dr. Martin: Tell me about it, I don't know about it.

Jane: Well, when we were first married he had an old friend,

INITIAL DIAGNOSTIC INTERVIEWS   99

and I guess that's all she was, an old friend; I thought it
was a girlfriend who used to call him up all the time; not
all the time, called him up a couple of times, and I thought
they were involved, they lived across the hall and she was
always sickening and lovey dovey and trying to make me
jealous and she did. She was . . . Jack had gotten married
and he was out of her reach now and she still wanted to be
interested in him and I never knew that he had any girlfriends; I didn't know who his girlfriends were. I knew that
he had a couple of girlfriends, but then after we were married, when this came up I imagined that he was being un-
faithful. It used to torment me so much, because I was so
paranoid at that time that I used to make up what was
happening when he was at school and I was at work and
that's all. So, that's when it all started. I felt justified in
calling up a friend of mine. ["Love-sick" wife with a paranoid trend.]

Dr. Martin: You experienced some slights, real or imagined ones.

Jane: No. I was just jealous.

Dr. Martin: You think you made them all up? He really didn't
do anything to hurt you?

Jane: No. I believe him now.

Dr. Martin: You've come a long way. That's very good. [At-
tempt at ego support following history of ego weakness.]

Jane: Except that I've gone and destroyed it all, his confidence
in me, by going out and having an affair. It's good for me,
but, it's bad for him. [Refuses support.]

Dr. Martin: Well, as I listen to him today, he sounds pretty good.
Are you hiding some of those feelings, you haven't told me?

Jack: The wounds are there; they are healing.

Dr. Martin: Tell me about the wounds.

Jack: The only thing is, and I try to get this across to her time
after time; we had a fight about this last night. I believe in
letting sleeping dogs lie at times and I consider myself to be
a sleeping dog in this. I'm perfectly willing to be forgiving
about this if we can drop the subject when dropping is
called for and clear the air when that is called for, but all
things being equal let's move on to other things and not
keep raking up the past. Just last night she mentioned that
her former lover had said that he wanted to keep her bare-
foot and pregnant and I wasn't doing this. She didn't want
to have to work for a living to suplement our budget and I
wasn't making enough money that she should be able to

devote all her time to the role of being wife and mother. I'll be damned if I'm going to do something for the sake of coming up to her erstwhile lover's expectations and that was it and that set me off; she knew it set me off, I told her what set me off and why and asked her for the umpteenth time to leave him out of this. If any progress is going to be made in the future it is going to be between her and me and not my trying to catch up with some ridiculous misconceptions of what this other person was like. She was living in a fantasy world at the time, I think that she'll admit it. Her opinion of this person was far afield of what he was doing, sort of a self-serving parasitic type person. So, yeah, I can get resentful at times, but only on specific basis.

Dr. Martin (to Jane): What are you thinking right now?

Jane: I was just thinking you're right. But sometimes it's hard for me, I mean I can't change a year's worth of wrong thinking. I admit now that I was wrong and living in my own fantasy world and that I had my poems and my songs and it was very romantic and all that; that there was no responsibility on either of our parts, but I just can't forget about that, I mean, the associations that naturally pop up aren't just going to go away. I'm sorry that I have to bring them up to you, you are not the right person to talk to, but who else is there to talk to about it.

Dr. Martin: Talk to me now, from now on. [Continuing emphasis on therapeutic relationship and contract.]

Jack: That's why we've been looking forward to this with great anticipation. The presence of a third party changes things a lot. Things when brought out to air in the presence of a third party have a tendency not to recur. Even if we've gone over it before and said the very same things to each other, it's kind of like having the whole thing witnessed.

Dr. Martin: You've both been very good and helpful. I've asked you many questions. Would you like to ask me any before we stop?

Jack: Not really. I'm satisfied with the course that things are taking.

Dr. Martin: All right, Jane, I will meet with you next Tuesday at 9:30, and Jack, I will meet with you next Wednesday at 9:30.

Jane: Thank you very much.

Jack: Thank you.

Although the initial diagnostic interview above contained all the elements that are essential for a tentative initial diagnosis and initial treatment plan, it was not necessary to reach a conclusion at this point. It was decided, therefore, to see each mate individually to refine the initial diagnoses and treatment plan.

The individual interview with Jane elaborated on the sexual history. Intimacy, both emotional and physical (love and sensuousness), were very important to her. She was very verbal and enjoyed long hours of talking together and lovemaking leading up to intercourse per se. The intercourse was not important to her and she rarely responded orgasmically. Thus she was unhappy with Jack who she claimed was unromantic and mechanical. She claimed that he was merely interested in intercourse and had progressively developed premature ejaculation and occasional impotence.

The thinking disorder recognized in the first interview was explored, and it was clear that when she was pressed, she would become confused and then angry. Her inability to depend consistently upon her thinking made it impossible for her to keep a full-time job or to perform consistently under pressure. This led to her original unspoken marriage contract that she would marry a rich boy from a wealthy, stable family (in contrast to her own) and would never have to work. Her poor judgment in believing that this was what marriage to Jack would be like set up an untenable reality for her. She had to leave him to look for an older wealthy man who would fulfill her contract. Her failure to accomplish this caused the emotional decompensation requiring hospitalization and a call to Jack to rescue her.

The individual interview with Jack again revealed him to be reluctant to look into himself. He did not think there was anything wrong with him. He was only here to help Jane. He was willing to suffer the pain (like his self-inflicted cuts) of Jane's mistreatment of him if she would stop complaining about him. He denied any validity to her complaints in any area (including sensual and emotional intimacy). It was clear how Jane's presence in the conjoint session forced him to face realities which he could deny in her absence. The dynamics of the development of the obsessional character or "cold-sick" husband which had been illustrated in the conjoint session continued to be exposed in the individual session. He was preoccupied with gaining control over himself and had succeeded in all areas, including control over feelings of warmth, intimacy, and love. He was hurt that the contract he had made with Jane was not honored by her. He had been a faithful, reliable husband, always helping her when she was in trouble. He felt that she was unfair, ungrateful, and continually hurting him. He admitted that he needed her because she was emotional, volatile, and brought liveliness and excitement into his life. He was willing to continue the marriage under his terms and felt Jane needed treatment to accept what he offered.

Marital Classification and Diagnosis

By *personality style and psychiatric terminology*:

Obssesive-compulsive husband and hysterical wife ("cold-sick" man and the "love-sick" woman).

By the *"normal" value system of diagnosis of marital disharmony*:

A. Individuality	Jack	Jane
1. Capacity for independence	yes	no
2. Capacity for supportiveness	yes	no
3. Capacity to accept support	no	yes
4. Capacity for lust	Failing	no
5. Capacity for sensuousness	no	yes
6. Capacity for love	no	no

B. *The Marriage Contract*

1. Conscious contract

a. Areas of agreement

They both had been lonely and socially unsuccessful and through the relationship expected companionship and not to be lonely anymore. The marriage would also satisfy social pressures (all their friends were getting married and their families expected it). The marriage would make them like other people. It would give them position and status in their own eyes as well as in those of people who were important to them.

b. Areas of disagreement

Prior to the marriage they had expressed no conscious areas of disagreement. This was because a dishonest contract was being written by both. Jane did not express her ideas of never working and of living without restrictions on money. They never discussed sexual needs, and her expectations that he would be a great lover were not discussed. Jack had no idea of Jane's expectations. He was planning on a safe, economic, comfortable job, with security as his primary objective. He also expected Jane to be able to work steadily to raise their economic base. He expected her to find him sexually satisfying as she seemed to feel prior to the marriage.

2. Unconscious contract

a. Areas of agreement

Both had felt themselves social failures with their peer groups and felt that in finding someone who would marry them, they could heal this wound. In this way, they were soulmates. (Note: had it not been for other conflicting drives they might have achieved a harmony due to dovetailing of needs as some couples do.)

b. Areas of disagreement

Jane expected her complete dependency to be accepted by Jack and to live blissfully in a state of eternal romantic love and paternal economic protection. She expected Jack to make her feel secure in her knowledge of herself as a female. In brief, she expected him to solve all of her problems because she felt she was incapable of doing this. Jack expected his defenses against being devastated by pain (which he had worked so hard to erect) would be respected. He expected to be loved and appreciated for doing his duty and that he be allowed to live a comfortable life, as his family had done, without disturbances over intimacy and love.

Therapeutic Formulation

The psychotherapeutic plan that was recommended was that each mate enter psychotherapy, using a combination of individual and conjoint couple-with-a-couple marital therapy. Jane was to see a woman therapist for work with her intrapsychic disorders and cognitive disability. The disturbed mother-child relationship was clear in Jane's history. Also, the female therapist would serve as a model showing the capability for work and love. Jack was to be seen by a male therapist to give him the support he needed and to lift his repression of all affect. When needed, the two therapists would meet with Jane and Jack to work out the marital difficulties that were interfering with the individual therapies.

A REALITY-ORIENTED METHOD OF CONDUCTING THE CONJOINT DIAGNOSTIC INTERVIEW

The following is presented as a model format for the initial conjoint marital interview as reported by Williams (1974). It is presented to illustrate one of the many different types of initial conjoint marital interviews. It is a systematic approach to diagnostic procedure and treatment plan development. It was designed to reduce the anxiety level in the initial interview and to elicit, in the shortest possible time, pertinent data from the dyad that is relevant to the history and present status of the marital relationship. This approach is based on the assumption that it is the relationship that is the "identified patient" in conjoint marital therapy. Although this is a limiting assumption, it serves its purpose well under conditions where the inner problems of either mate prevent the focus on the relationship.

This diagnostic approach resulted from an adaptation of sociological studies that identified the major common areas of adjustment in successfully married couples (Landis, 1946, and Terman, 1938). Williams considered the essential indicators of adjustment to be (1) an effective and functioning communication system within the marriage dyad, and (2) a high level of agreement between husband and wife concerning shared feelings and attitudes in each of the identified areas.

Step 1. Preparation of the Couple for Information Giving

The purpose here is to erase misperceptions as to the nature of the process and to lower the anxiety states in an effort to solicit more correct information in the following step.

A. The role of the therapist is explained as one whose purpose is to help all present gain insight into the problems of the relationship —not as one who is there to judge or penalize.

B. The marriage is identified as the patient. The partners are asked to help, as co-therapists, as all look at the patient—the marriage.

C. The following inventory is introduced in an informal way.

Step 2. Taking the Marital Inventory

The six areas of the inventory, when thoroughly explored, should reveal a "complete" history and present status of the marriage. Throughout the inventory it is essential that the therapist be aware of the level of communication and agreement or disagreement of the partners.

A. *Religion*

1. Family religious background
2. Present views *of the couple* with regard to religion
3. Discernment of values, life goals, etc., of each partner and degree of similarity between the two. Object: to find out if the couple presents a *unified* philosophy of life.

B. *Friends*

1. Ability of the couple to distinguish his friends, her friends, and their friends.
2. Extent of agreement concerning feelings and attitudes towards all three classes of friends. Object: to ascertain ability of the couple to differentiate the three types of friends in marriage and the degree of shared attitudes concerning the friends.

C. *In-laws*

1. Perceived effect of in-law relations upon marriage.
2. Attitudes of each concerning in-law relations.
3. Degree of consensus concerning feelings toward in-laws. Object: to determine the extent to which the couple agrees concerning the feelings and attitudes towards the in-laws and whether or not those stated feelings and attitudes are in fact employed by the couple as a unit in dealing with the in-laws.

D. *Activities*

1. Feelings and attitudes of each toward the vocational activities of themselves and of their partner.
2. Feelings and attitudes of each toward the avocational activities of themselves and of their partner.
3. General idea of time allotment to separate vocational and avocational activities.
4. General idea of time allotment to shared vocational and avocational activities.
5. Ability to identify positive or negative feelings towards any of the above. Object: (1) ascertainment of general time allotment for activities, and (2) exploration of feeling level and content for each activity.

E. *Budget*

1. Attitude toward income level.
2. Attitude toward spending and/or saving level.
3. Agreement as to specific allocation of income.
4. Exploration of the "mechanics" of decision making and purchasing of major items.
5. Money management patterns in each family of origin. Object: to determine to what extent the partners agree as a couple on the generation and expenditure of income and to try to elicit subjective feelings in this area.

F. *Sex*

1. Degree of agreement as to the present adequacy of the conjugal relationship *without regard to specifics* such as frequency, position, etc. Object: to determine the *present* level of satisfaction for each partner with the marital sexual adjustment.

Step 3. Recapitulation for the Partners

Close the interview by summarizing the information that has come to light. Point out the apparent strengths of the relationship and indicate the areas in which communication of feelings and consensus of attitudes seem to be blocked.

Step 4. Formation of the Treatment Plan

The therapist should have an adequate conception of the present status of the marital relationship and be able to make an accurate assessment of the status of the communication system. What remains is to devise a treatment plan setting up as primary objectives those items within the various areas which appear to be the major items causing communication dysfunction and which are the major obstacles to successful adjustment.

It is interesting to note that in both types of initial interviews, though they differ greatly in content of information, the attempt is made to locate the areas of matching needs and expectations and the areas between the mates which will likely constitute the substance of the future therapy sessions.

TOWARD THE SELECTION OF THERAPY

The initial diagnostic interviews, when completed, lead naturally to a decision whether or not to recommend treatment and, if treatment is recommended, which type of therapy is most suitable for the presenting problem. Instead of taking up this subject next, I will wait until I have described, in the next chapter, the wide variety of choices available for treatment of marital problems.

REFERENCES

Berman, E. M., and Lief, H. I. (1975), Marital therapy from a psychiatry perspective: and overview. *American Journal of Psychiatry*, 132, 6: 583-592.

Bird, H. W., and Martin, P. A. (1956), Countertransference in the psychotherapy of marriage partners. *Psychiatry*, 19: 353-360.

Erikson, E. (1968), *Identity, Youth and Crisis.* New York: W. W. Norton and Co.

Gill, M., Newman, R., and Redlich, F. C. (1954), *The Initial Interview in Psychiatric Practice.* New York: International Universities Press.

Group for the Advancement of Psychiatry (1973), *Assessment of Sexual Function: A Guide to Interviewing.* New York: Mental Health Materials Center.

Howells, J. G. (1975), *Principles of Family Psychiatry.* New York: Brunner/Mazel, p. 177.

Kaplan, H. S. (1974), *The New Sex Therapy.* New York: Brunner/Mazel.

Knox, D. (1971), *Marriage Happiness.* Champaign, Illinois: Research Press, p. 2.

Landis, J. T. (1946), Length of time required to achieve adjustment in marriage. *American Sociological Review*, 11: 666-678.

Lowry, T. S., and Lowry, T. P. (1975), Ethical considerations in sex therapy, *Journal of Marriage and Family Counseling*, 1: 229-236.

MacKinnon, R. A., and Michels, R. (1971), *The Psychiatric Interview in Clinical Practice.* Philadelphia: W. B. Saunders Co., p. 7.

Martin, P. A. (1957), The kaleidoscopic nature of psyche and soma. *Journal of the Michigan State Medical Society*, 56: 1249-1251.

Saul, L. F. (1957), The psychoanalytic diagnostic interview. *The Psychoanalytic Quarterly*, 26: 76-90.

Spoerl, O. H. (1975), Abstract: single session in psychotherapy. *Diseases of the Nervous System*, 36, 6: 283-285.

Story, N. L. (1974), Sexual dysfunction resulting from drug side effects. *The Journal of Sex Research*, 10: 132-149.

Terman, L. (1938), *Psychological Factors in Marital Happiness*. New York: McGraw-Hill Book Company.

Williams, A. R. (1974), The initial conjoint marital interview: one procedure. *The Family Coordinator*, 23, 4: 391-397.

6

Techniques of Marital Therapy

IN THIS CHAPTER I will attempt to combine an historical presentation of the development of marital therapy (to show the sweep and movement of the field) together with a listing of the advantages and disadvantages of the many techniques. The relatively recent flood of new treatment techniques makes it impossible even to mention every one of them, let alone elaborate on the method of using each one.

Psychotherapy of marital problems was officially recognized as a designated form of psychotherapy about fifty years ago in America (Olson, 1970). It is only within the last few decades that a separate profession has developed to treat couples who were experiencing difficulties in their marital relationship. However, as long as psychotherapy has been practiced, marital therapy has been involved, whether or not it was so designated. For example, in their important study of the married in treatment, Sager et al. (1968) observed that marital difficulties may prompt as many as 50 percent of patients to seek treatment. In the other 50 percent, recognition of a major marital problem may develop in the course of analysis in as high as 25 percent of the analysands. The intimate nature of the marital relationship, reproducing and surpassing in intensity even that of the infant-mother relationship, is a natural situation for the development and expression of disturbed interpersonal relations. The same holds true for any intimate relationship, whether legally designated as marital or not.

THE CLASSICAL APPROACH—PSYCHOANALYSIS

The classical approach to the treatment of marriage partners is for the therapist to take the mate who has designated himself as the patient into psychoanalysis, and never to see the spouse. The spouse may never enter treatment. Psychoanalysis is a dyadic type of treatment based on an intense one-to-one relationship between patient and therapist. It is based on the concepts of free association, interpretation, transference, resistance, and unconscious mental activity. The patient free associates, the analyst interprets. The development of the transference neurosis and its interpretation is the cornerstone of the analysis. All efforts are directed to keep the transference neurosis free from contaminations such as the analyst seeing the spouse. The greatest concern most analysts hold about seeing the spouse is that these communications will endanger the trust and confidence that the patient puts in the analyst. Success in therapy depends on the patient-analyst relationship, making confidentiality crucial.

If a therapeutic alliance can be established between the conflict-free portion of the patient's ego and the analyst, a two on one advantage over the conflicted portion of the patient contributes to success. Resolution of immobilizing transference-countertransference deadlocks leads to successful change in the patient's psychodynamics. In the classical approach, change in the marital relationship is viewed as dependent upon, or incidental to, the main changes in the analysand's psychodynamics. Despite the focus on the individual rather than on the marriage partners, analysis does catalyze toward an improved marital relationship; improvement in the mental health of one spouse is positively correlated with improvement in the well-being of the other (Sager et al., 1968). One result of analysis is to help patients move toward a resolution of an unhappy marital state—more often to improve rather than to dissolve the marriage.

Successful resolution of the marriage problems by this method necessitates a patient with basic ego strengths which allow for structural changes and continuing problem solving without dependency upon an initiating change in the marriage partner or even a positive response to the change from the partner. With the successful analysis of such a person, with the mate never having entered into treatment, one of several results has been observed: (1) The analysand has psychodynamically separated and individuated and is now capable of successful functioning in the marriage even if previously desired unfulfilled dependency needs or expectations are still not being gratified by the mate, who may or may not have been in need of change. A one-way change has occurred in the marriage sufficient to make the individual and the marriage functional. (2) The change in the analysand has brought about a change in the responses of the mate and a new, successful type of relationship is established.

(3) In about 7 percent of cases, the mate responds by developing serious psychological disturbances as the patient improves (Sager et al., 1968). In these cases, the improvement of the mate in separate treatment causes a shift in the pathological equilibrium, with a resultant decompensation in the untreated mate. This may necessitate treatment, contribute to a divorce, or add new burdens for the successfully treated partner to carry. In a study focused specifically on the pathological reactions or psychiatric illnesses of marital partners precipitated by clinical improvement or recovery of the patient, Kohl (1962) made some important observations. Not only did these mates' reactions to recovery of the patient constitute serious obstacles to the continued recovery of the patients, but they occurred as illnesses severe enough to necessitate active treatment for themselves. Another important observation was that it was not uncommon or surprising to find that the less sick marital partner had been the first to seek treatment voluntarily, but without awareness of the pathological nature of their marital adjustment. (4) The change in the analysand without accompanying change in the mate leads to an "impossible situation," with resultant divorce instigated by one or the other of the married couple (usually by the treated partner who has gained the strength to make this move).

When the analysis is unsuccessful a number of different outcomes are possible: (1) The marriage continues in its previous disturbed pattern. (2) The "untreated" mate has used the patient's analysis creatively and, based on these changes, a new and better relationship is established. Mates often make positive transferences to the unseen therapist through which they effect changes not made by the one in treatment. When the transference is negative the mate will work to destroy the therapeutic efforts of the therapeutic dyad. (3) Divorce may occur in an effort by the former analysand to attribute his lack of change and his personal difficulties to the disturbed marriage. Or (4) the mate, having waited during treatment in hope of a change, now chooses divorce.

Advantages

1. The patient is the patient (in contrast to the marriage being the patient). The patient takes the responsibility for personal change, growth, and development (intrapsychic change); for problem solving in the marriage (interpersonal change); and for constructive changes in reality (in the marriage or otherwise).

2. With resolution of the childhood neurosis and the transference neurosis, the same themes in the marriage neurosis can now be resolved.

3. This is the second most successful technique where divorce is the chosen solution by one of the partners (Cookerly, 1973). As stated by Greene et al. (1965), one spouse has to figure out his own way, irrespective of the consequences to the mate.

4. This method is protective of any "secrets" that the patient wishes permanently hidden from the mate (e.g., homosexuality, infidelity, or a painful failure, such as dishonorable discharge from the army or a past criminal offense).

It has been stated that these "so-called" family secrets are known, either consciously or unconsciously, by the partner and that premature discussion of the secret could disrupt the marriage (Greene, 1970). It has been my experience, however, that there are some mates who do not know consciously or unconsciously of the "so-called" secret. Insistence on disclosure of the "secret" by a therapist would be an indiscriminate application of a rule of thumb. There is a common clinical entity of a mate who comes to the therapist for help to tell the partner of a current affair. The patient complains of feeling very guilty, and confessing the affair to the mate would be guilt relieving. The picture is one of placing the responsibility for problem solving onto the mate. Sometimes the patient wishes to be able then to continue the affair and also have the marriage through the mate's capacity for understanding which is to be aided by the therapist. At other times the purpose is to have the mate break up the affair because the patient feels too weak to do so independently. Therapeutically there are some "secrets" to be handled by the patient alone, which contributes to personal growth and development.

The therapist must carefully evaluate each mate's desire for disclosure of secrets and capacity to adjust to the disclosed secrets. There are wide variations in these factors.

5. This method is advantageous with that type of person whose dynamics demand exclusive attention from the therapist and who could not work in conjoint or group settings. In this category are patients whose problems of narcissism demand total attention for themselves; those with marked sibling rivalry problems; and one type of paranoid patient who does not trust the mate or fears collusion between therapist and mate.

6. Advantages are apparent where both mates have different goals in terms of their marriage problem and seek help for independent solutions.

Disadvantages

1. Length of time involved.
2. Limited availability of psychoanalysis.
3. Limited suitability of many patients.
4. Therapist must rely on a patient's account of the interactions with his mate (with the necessity to recognize distortions, denials, projective identifications, omissions, and conscious lying) and at the same time avoid the opportunity for firsthand observations of these transactions.
5. A lack of early inclusion of the marital partner in the total treatment plan, as occurs in classical therapy, may lead to consequences of premature termination of the patient's treatment or failure to avoid the development of a serious illness in the marital partner. Kohl (1962) states that when pathological reactions of marital partners appear to be complementary, the patient's therapist must give due consideration to his responsibility for the well-being of the untreated partner.

6. Kubie (1965) observed that, when confronted with a marital crisis, it was hard for the analyst to decide whether or not to undertake an analysis at all, because no matter how successful the analysis, the outcome of the marriage would depend, in part, on the ultimate attitude of the untreated partner.

7. When the marital problems surface after the individual has entered analysis, an early referral of the partner for individual treatment is indicated, but the lack of communication between the therapists often delays understanding of what is really happening in the marital situation. Projective identifications cloud the material, making it difficult and sometimes impossible for therapy to progress.

8. Classical treatment is disadvantageous with the type of patient who plans to control the input of material and does not want the mate presenting material to the therapist which will give control of the therapy to the therapist.

9. When the mate of the patient in analysis has disturbing paranoid reactions about the analysis, classical analysis may not be the treatment of choice. The mate may need to know every detail of every hour, with resultant repeated questioning. The fear is that of being "told on" or being influenced by the mate in treatment.

Indications

This approach is not indicated for treatment of marital problems per se. It is indicated for treatment of the married person who seeks help primarily for himself or herself and who is ego strong and capable of accepting the responsibility for the solution of the marital disharmony through inner changes, whether the mate changes or not. It is also indicated where the designated patient is the stronger of the two mates; also where privacy and confidentiality are necessary for successfully treating a disturbed marriage.

Giovacchini (1965) and Drellich (1968) prefer the classic psychoanalytic approach with separate analysts in marital disharmony. Theoretically, in the carefully selected couple, this would be the ideal solution. In practice, the field of marital therapy has moved away from this position. Giovacchini's emphasis on the initial mother-child symbiosis being repeated in the marital symbiosis does illustrate, however, the depth of therapy necessary for successful treatment of some types of marital problems.

Contraindications

This approach is contraindicated where the marital crisis is so severe that it demands that the *marriage* become the immediate patient and not one of the mates.

CONSECUTIVE PSYCHOTHERAPY

We begin our historical survey of the literature illustrating changing attitudes toward seeing the spouse with the work of a renowned psychoanalyst, Clarence Oberndorf, the pioneer in marital therapy. In 1931, he presented a paper stressing the importance of the marital relationship in symptom formation. This was followed by a paper (Oberndorf, 1934) describing a case of a couple with *folie à deux*. They held in common similar paranoid symptoms. Their relationship remained harmonious by having a common enemy, reality. In contrast to marital disharmony, overt symptoms were directed out against the world instead of toward each other. He later published an article on married couples whom he had analyzed by treating each spouse in succession (Oberndorf, 1938). This psychotherapeutic technique is called Consecutive Dyadic Psychotherapy.

Advantages

1. The experience of consecutive analyses offers the therapist an understanding that may not have been clear to him during the first mate's analysis. The therapist recognizes in retrospect those areas of conflict which the first analysand had avoided. Conscious and unconscious deceptive mechanisms used during the first mate's treatment are uncovered.

2. The second analysis promotes an understanding of how the partners in the marriage communicate unconsciously and how they support their complementary neuroses.

3. The second mate's analysis benefits from the work in the first analysis; from the first hour, the therapist has an understanding of this

mate from the knowledge derived during the first analysis as well as the helpful knowledge of the first mate in treatment.

4. Since the marriage neurosis repeats the original infantile neurosis, clarification of each is aided by the therapist's advantageous viewpoint.

Disadvantages

1. The length of time involved before the second mate gets into treatment.

2. Negative reactions of first mate to loss of therapist during second mate's analysis.

3. Second mate's anxieties about allegiance of therapist to first mate.

4. Countertransference reactions in therapist contributing to favoring one mate over the other.

Indications

1. Where completion of first analysis has not resulted in the establishment of a stable equilibrium in the marriage and both partners wish the second mate to enter treatment with the therapist to achieve this result.

Contraindications

1. Where one of the mates is opposed to use of same therapist.

2. Where one of the mates is seeking a divorce and the other mistakenly believes the treatment is for the purpose of perpetuating the marriage.

CONCURRENT PSYCHOTHERAPY

Bela Mittlemann's work (1944, 1948, 1956), following a decade of apparent overlooking of Oberndorf's publications, opened the door for a flood of experimentation with new approaches to the treatment of marriage partners, experimentation that is continuing in intensity to this day. The explosion in the literature is due to the fact that many related and varying disciplines have contributed to the increasing knowledge about the treatment of marital dyads. Extension of

Freudian intrapsychic dynamics occurred within psychoanalysis and other areas of psychiatry, and the other behavioral sciences opened broad vistas of knowledge about marital interaction and treatment of marital disorders. Mittelmann, like Oberndorf, noted that the neuroses of husband and wife complement each other and that there is a dovetailing of conflictual and defensive patterns. Some of these complementary reactions afford relief for the patient; others are of such a type as to perpetuate and renew the pathologic reactions. Mittelmann's contributions went beyond Oberndorf's in stressing more forcefully the significance to psychotherapy of the mates' interrelationship and the advantage of this method to the therapist. This method helped him to see both the reality and the neurotically determined interactions between mates. Also, the method helped him to pick up trends that might be missed when only one partner reported to him.

Advantages (from Mittelmann, 1948)

1. The analyst obtains a more complete picture of the realities and of complementary reactions of the two individuals.

2. Information may be obtained from one that the other does not reveal or underplays to such an extent that the analyst might fail to recognize some crucial trends.

3. By gauging the relative risks involved in the changing reactions of one or the other, the analyst can increase or lessen the emphasis of his interpretations.

4. Through the change of one mate, the analyst alters a reality which presented insurmountable difficulties to the other. The correction of these difficulties relieves the patient's helplessness and increases his confidence in the therapist. This allows the patient to face his inner problems.

Disadvantages

1. Disadvantages revolve about transference and countertransference problems which are complicated by this technique.

2. Where either mate cannot accept the confidential nature of the information given to the therapist and is afraid it will be divulged.

3. Where the mates cannot avoid discussing each other's analyses.

Indications (from Greene, 1970)

1. Where the power structure is such that one mate has overwhelmed the other.
2. Where insight into their behavior patterns as they affect each partner is needed to produce changes in behavior. Highlighting of the interpersonal aspects has become essential for treatment.
3. One or both of the mates have the capacity for intensive exploration and change of intrapsychic, interpersonal and environmental forces.

Contraindications

1. Presence of severe psychosis or severe character disorders in one or both spouses.
2. Marked-to-severe paranoid reactions with suspicious attitudes toward the communications of the mate.
3. Excessive sibling rivalry conflicts that prevent sharing the therapist.
4. Family secrets whose exposure could not be tolerated by one of the mates.
5. Whenever therapy could precipitate a severe regressive phenomenon because of fragile defenses in one spouse.

HISTORICAL INTERLUDE

The publications of Mittelmann were a sign of the ferment that was taking place in psychoanalysis. His work was in keeping with enlargement of focus, as was the work of Harry Stack Sullivan (1953) and his concept of interpersonal relations. This movement brought the marital problems of the patient into sharper focus. In Great Britain W. R. Fairbairn (1952) elaborated an object relations theory of personality which H. V. Dicks (1952, 1963) utilized to develop a multifaceted approach to marital relations, their pathology, and their treatment. The influence of his work on marital therapy did not reach America until later (Dicks, 1967). This has resulted in an object-relations approach to psychotherapy with marital couples. In this approach couples in conflict are viewed as more similar than dissimilar despite apparent differences; the therapist's countertransference reactions are seen not as irrational but as a valid reflection of the patient's struggle; the adult or child who is the identified patient is often a carrier or container of the split-off, unacceptable impulses of the other; the individual is perceived as part of a unit in which even the most obvious pathological traits have an inherent healthy reparative function (Stewart, et al., 1975).

A Collaborative Approach

The first paper of Martin and Bird, whose approach is discussed here, was limited solely to the description of a new technique of treating marriage partners. Each partner is seen by a different psychiatrist in psychotherapy. The Stereoscopic Technique (Martin and Bird, 1953), as used in collaborative psychotherapy of marriage partners, consists of planned, regular reviews of the two psychiatrists' reconstructed versions of important events in the lives of the marriage partners. This approach allowed for an immediate recognition of distortions of reality in the productions of the patients. Such recognitions led to understanding of the distinguishing ego defenses and the instinctual impulses that were being warded off in each mate. The authors started working together because they discovered that in a number of patients with whom they were working the classical psychoanalytic technique was not usable by the marriage partner who first became a patient. They were too emotionally disturbed, too involved with their mates, and lacked the ego strength necessary for dyadic psychoanalytic therapy. In these patients, the neurotic symptoms, conflicts, or regressions were not only fixed in their own personality, but were, in addition, maintained by powerful emotional forces in the marriage partner to whom the patient was bound. For example, neurotic symptoms or regression to a psychosis may be the choice of one marriage partner in preference to separation from or murder of the so-called normal mate. Thus, the therapeutic action of the analysis of the initial patient was made impossible by the needs and activities of the mate.

By comparing the productions of mates, the psychiatrists could understand the complementary neuroses that existed between the partners, which both drew them together and pulled them apart. The study of the current relationships between the spouses and the transference neuroses in the individual therapies made possible the reconstruction of even the earliest symbiotic and separation phases of infant-mother relationships. Thus, the therapeutic approach in the individual therapies was basically psychoanalytically conventional, but a sharper focus on the interpersonal and reality factors added new therapeutic dimensions. Clarification of the marriage neurosis came more quickly and clearly. In addition, a new relationship between the psychiatrists was added as was an added transference from each patient to the mate's psychiatrist.

The collaborative approach is a psychoanalytic approach between therapist and patient with an additional relation between the two therapists which highlights countertransference reactions of the psychiatrists to their individual patients.

Advantages

1. The therapist is freed from a single observation post, giving a broader perspective of the patient within his natural setting.

2. Distortions of reality and projective identifications are more readily recognized as well as some which might never have been recognized.

3. Reduction of anxiety and cessation of destructive behavior is effected in one or both partners through their knowledge that the therapists are working together.

4. It allows for the observation of the unconscious reactions of one partner to the unconscious actions of the other and illuminates the marriage neurosis, the infantile neurosis, and the transference.

5. The uniqueness of this technique from those described up to this point in the historical survey is its built-in safety factor of one therapist revealing the other's countertransference reactions which could interfere with the progress of the therapy. The use of one therapist as a check upon the other is invaluable technically in preventing transference-counter transference deadlocks in therapy.

6. It is advantageous to the therapists' continuing growth and development since it eliminates the disadvantages of isolation.

Disadvantages to the Psychotherapist

1. Loss of time. Utilization of the approach demands regular planned conferences between the therapists. This can be a realistic problem.

2. The therapist faces an added task of working out what can be a difficult and sensitive relationship with his colleague.

Disadvantages to the Patient

1. There is an intrusion upon the development of the doctor-patient relationship by the psychiatrist-psychiatrist relationship. This is the most serious disadvantage to the patient.

2. Change in the availability of one of the therapists breaks up the prearranged usage of the technique.

Indications

1. Opposition of one mate to being treated by the same therapist as the other mate. Need for an individual therapist.

2. A negative reaction (hostility) of one mate toward the therapist.

3. Referral from another therapist because of his discomfort or lack of familiarity with a conjoint or concurrent technique.

4. Referral from another therapist because one mate has created therapeutic complications or because the mates have widely different goals in therapy.

Contraindications

1. When one mate cannot tolerate not knowing what is happening in the other mate's therapy.

2. When the two therapists involved have difficulty in communication, rivalry or power problems and cannot use the opportunity as a continuing education and growth experience.

SIMULTANEOUS THERAPY

I note the approach described by Alexander Thomas (1956) on simultaneous psychotherapy with marital partners, not because it was a new technique but because it illustrates a shift in emphasis illustrative of changes in the literature taking place at about this time. He reported favorable results with simultaneous analytic psychotherapy of marital partners in selected cases with a modification of the usual analytic procedure in the direction of using the interpersonal relationship between the partners instead of the relationship with the therapist as the prime focus for the delineation of the neurotic patterns and the initiation of change. This modification was made possible by the therapist's accurate knowledge of the interplay between husband and wife through his contact with both. Therapeutic attention is shifted from the patient-therapist relationship to the family relationship. By 1954, a dramatic shift had taken place; whereas formerly a therapist could not afford to consider the family, now he could not afford to neglect the family.

During the 1950's, techniques and theories were evolved as a result of advances in child psychiatry which opened new vistas to the understanding of psychodynamics, personality development, and the perpetuation of psychopathology (Sager, 1966a). These were soon translated into new approaches in marital therapy. Among these advances were the concept of the double bind by Bateson, Jackson, Haley, and Weakland (1956); Spiegel's (1957) model of role conflict in the family; Jackson (1957) on family homeostasis; Wynne's (1958) theory of pseudomutuality; and Ackerman's (1958) pioneering studies of the family.

CONJOINT MARITAL THERAPY

Conjoint marital therapy (Jackson, 1957) involves both mates in the same session with the therapist. Conjoint marital therapy brought the larger issues of family therapy into the picture since children, if present in the marriage, were included in the therapy. Don Jackson first introduced the term conjoint therapy, although Mittelmann first used this technique, and the literature of social workers shows use of this method before Mittelmann. Jackson defined conjoint marital therapy as a therapeutic method in which both marital partners are seen together by the same therapist or co-therapists, one male and one female, and in which the signaling symptom or condition is viewed by the therapist as a comment on the dysfunction of their interactional system (Jackson and Weakland, 1961). In this approach, the patient is seen by the therapist as a family-surrounded individual with real life problems in the present day. This and the associated idea that the patient is enmeshed in a fixed scheme of behavior where each family member is expected to behave in a mutually accepted way result in differences between the psychoanalytic intrapsychic approach and this interpersonal psychotherapeutic approach. It is an operational approach based on the postulate that the interpersonal relationships involve two levels of communication allowing for double bind relationships. Virginia Satir (1965) and Andrew Watson (1962) contributed to the early literature on conjoint marital therapy. A detailed description of one therapist's understanding and method of conducting conjoint marital therapy is presented by R. V. Fitzgerald (1973), using clinical vignettes of what takes place in the therapy room.

It is obvious of course that a psychotherapist can see both marriage partners at the same time and use the traditional psychoanalytic approach and it would still be called conjoint therapy. It would be a dyadic therapy, but the emphasis would be on the transference analysis and not on the interactional analysis of Don Jackson. In addition, with the application of more recent developments, techniques of behavior therapy or general systems approach may be the major emphasis in the conjoint sessions.

The conjoint method of marital therapy is the most frequently used of the several different techniques described.

Advantages

1. Effective, convenient, and economical for single therapist and mates.

2. Contributes to development of dialogue between the mates (communication skills).

3. Quicker and greater access to dynamics of the marriage.

4. Provides access to conscious and unconscious aspects of marital contract whose mutual strivings and interdependent needs can be reinforced and whose distrust and hostilities can be ameliorated if not totally eliminated.

5. Gives mates advantage of heightened perceptions.

6. Gives therapist advantage of: (a) direct observation of the participants, allowing (b) more objective evaluation of the partners' behavior (limiting the need to judge distortion from more distant data) and (c) observation of the healthier sides of the marriage, (d) opportunity for constructive setting of limits of the marriage which enables the therapist to structure the marriage for the exploration of variables underlying the disharmony.

7. Places leverage on both mates to re-examine their reality testing and indirectly provide the therapist with "co-therapists."

Disadvantages

1. Mates may present a united front to defeat the therapist's efforts to effect change.

2. Mates may have differing goals such as one seeking divorce and the other continuation of the marriage. Conjoint therapy tends more toward perpetuating the marriage than some of the other techniques such as individual, consecutive, concurrent, or collaborative marital therapy.

Indications (from Greene, 1970)

1. Therapeutic impasse with concurrent approach.

2. Paranoid or suspicious behavior of one mate who becomes disturbed without reassuring knowledge of what transpired in other mate's individual session, requiring conjoint sessions.

3. Economic factors not allowing for individual therapy for each mate.

4. Explosiveness of marital situation such as physical abuse, which requires speed in bringing controls to the marriage.

5. Marriages in which there are problems which are largely acting out in nature.

6. Marriages where the need for establishing communications is predominant.

7. Marriages in which one or both mates have a cognitive disorder interfering with perceiving relationships between events and their own responses, thus necessitating immediate confrontation by the therapist as the events occur between the couples in the therapeutic hour.

Contraindications

1. *Folie à deux*. Separation of spouses results in gradual subsiding of psychotic picture in dependent spouse.

2. When one spouse has a severe psychosis necessitating separation and hospitalization. In some cases of hysterical psychoses occurring as a reaction to the marital partner, separation from the mate contributes to a remartialing of forces and a subsiding of the psychotic reaction (Martin, 1971).

3. Excessive narcissistic attitudes of one mate whose problems demand individual therapy.

4. An unexposable secret in one mate.

COMBINED APPROACH OF GREENE, SOLOMON, AND LUSTIG (1960)

This approach makes use of individual, concurrent, collaborative, and conjoint sessions when, in the opinion of the therapist, both triadic and dyadic transactions are necessary either for successful treatment of the marital transaction or of one of the partners. The approach is very flexible and lends itself to the styles of various therapists and to the personalities and situations of various married couples (Greene, 1970). Their approach, as different from the classical psychoanalytic, was based on the transactional concept of the nature of marital disharmony; homeostatic transactions become characteristic of a marriage (Greene, Broadhurst, and Lustig, 1965). This was again a shift away from classical psychoanalysis. However, they still dealt with transference reactions (a *triangular* transference neurosis) and also psychoanalytically studied projective identifications in the marital tensions.

Their treatment process in the combined techniques is based on a plan of active support, including environmental manipulation, complementary goals, clarification of role expectations and enactments, redirection of intrapersonal energies, and evocation of "healthier" communication. It not only combined techniques but also theoretical considerations. They added to the recognition and utilization of transference phenomena in the conjoint sessions two additional "triangular" transference transactions. First is the triangular transference neurosis—the reproduction of the oedipal constellation. Here is observed an interplay of a variety of roles that patients take in relation to one another and to the therapist that are variations of mother, father, and child and/or adolescent. They use transference dreams to further illuminate the nature of these roles through the introjective and projective mechanisms which appear in them.

Advantages

1. Extreme responsiveness to changing current needs of the marital partners based on a recognition of wide variability in marital patterns and unpredictability of therapeutic courses.
2. Many of the advantages described previously for collaborative and conjoint techniques.
3. The added advantages resulting from concurrent, individual, family, and group therapy.
4. Increases the perceptive awareness of therapist and patients.
5. Allows therapist to observe the varying reactions of the individual to different environments, thus serving as a corrective for the therapeutic misperceptions and misinterpretations.

Disadvantages

1. Hollender (1971) has voiced the most salient disadvantage of the combined technique. If the plan of therapy is not made explicit to the patients and if rules are changed *ad lib*, the result with some couples can be confusion. He warns of the potential for the kind of harm caused by the old shotgun prescription.

Indications

Greene (1970) lists the following indications for the simple combined and the combined-collaborative techniques:
1. Initial evaluation indicates triadic sessions to manage the marital relationship in order to achieve harmony, and dyadic sessions for entrenched personal conflicts.
2. Therapeutic impasse with other techniques.
3. Acting out by one or both mates that cannot be dealt with by the other techniques.

4. One mate's rigid personality pattern that makes it necessary to enlist the cooperation of the partner.

5. One mate's dynamics make dyadic setting too threatening.

6. An impasse in concurrent therapy because of transference difficulties.

7. A therapeutic impasse occurs in dyadic interviews because the dyadic transference neurosis can be activated and interpreted only in triadic sessions.

Contraindications

Similar to those previously listed for conjoint therapy.

THE FAMILY APPROACH

Nathan Ackerman in his definitive work on the family advocated a psychotherapeutic approach to the family as a family (Ackerman, 1958). This is not an approach of individual psychotherapy for each member; Ackerman contemplated a direct therapy of the family group and advocated the psychoanalytic interpretation of unconscious dynamics in their social context. This approach emphasizes the growth in the analyst's reality testing as well worth the increased complications of the transferences.

The entire field of family therapy is new and changing rapidly. There is a tendency for therapists to polarize into two approaches: those who view the family as a complicating factor in any individual member's intrapsychic struggles and those who view the transactions of the family as determining, in a dynamic way, the responses and attitudes of its members (GAP, 1970). Ackerman's work influenced marital therapy techniques and can best be illustrated as stated by him. (Ackerman, 1958, p. 151): "A relationship represents more than the sum of two personalities. A new level of organization creates new qualities. A marital relationship, like a chemical compound, has unique qualities of its own, over and above the characteristics of the elements that merge to form the compound." In marital therapy recognition of the positive values of utilizing these unique qualities has contributed to therapeutic efficacy.

Treatment of the Couple by a Couple (Conjoint Therapy)

The change in technical and theoretical emphasis shown in the preceding historical development is clearly illustrated in the work of Georges R. Reding and co-workers. (Reding and Ennis, 1964; Reding et al., 1967). They describe the treatment of a couple by a couple in the same session, which is a variation of conjoint therapy. Their original model of four-way treatment of marital couples in 1964 viewed it as a combination of two individual treatments. Their 1967 publication shows a change in emphasis both in treatment and in theory. They now emphasize the relationship between the patient couple and the therapist couple, rather than the individual relationships of the four participants; and also the impact of the patient couple's communications upon the relationship between the two therapists. They pay specific attention to the current thoughts and affective reactions of the therapists toward each other. They make extensive use of transference and countertransference interpretations from couple to couple during the four-way sessions. Their combination of the psychoanalytical model (transference and countertransference) and psychodrama (interpretations are acted out before they are verbalized) limits the intensity of the transference neurosis which the patient couple can develop with the therapist couple. This is in keeping with their treatment goal which is to open up channels of communication between the partners rather than to foster a maturation of their respective personalities. They substitute a different way of behaving and communicating with each other for deeper insight by each individual. A later development of this technique has been the use of a therapy couple who are married to each other. This furthers the modeling role of the therapist couple, particularly in the area of open communication between patient couples.

Advantages

1. The mix of a male and a female therapist brings to the fore additional material and behavior to be observed.

2. A means is provided of tapping the already present strengths of an older relationship (the patients') in order to solve current difficulties.

3. This type of marital therapy is also a powerful technique for the treatment of various individual disorders because of the use that is made of the marital relationship and the influence of each of the partners upon the other as a therapeutic agent.

4. The advantages of conjoint therapy mentioned previously in this chapter.

5. Intensification and acceleration of psychotherapeutic processes (Gill and Temperly, 1974).

Disadvantages

1. Same as for conjoint therapy mentioned previously in this chapter.

2. The relationship between the patient couple must be a healthy one and as free as possible from neurotic acting out or inhibitions which limit communication.

Indications

1. Where therapist couple is comfortable working together.

2. Where patient couple can use modeling approach more effectively than depth interpretation.

Contraindications

1. Inability of therapist couple to work constructively together.

2. Where one of the patients cannot work in the presence of a member of the same sex or opposite sex in the treatment session.

HISTORICAL INTERLUDE—GROUP THERAPY

During the 1950's, interest in group therapy stemmed from psychoanalytic considerations, particularly in London. Bion, in attempting to apply psychoanalytic understanding to experimental groups at Tavistock Clinic, found that he could delineate phenomenological patterns of group action (Bion, 1961). Ezriel elaborated group theory and method by attempting to gauge group interaction in terms of the unconscious common group tension, or the unconscious psychodynamic pattern, that the group was trying to deal with at a particular moment (Ezriel, 1950). A concurrent interest in psychoanalytic group therapy occurred in America and was soon utilized by marital therapists.

MARRIED COUPLE GROUP THERAPY

Neubeck in the early 1950's reported on married couple groups therapy (Neubeck, 1954) and was followed by many reports in the 1960's (Leichter, 1962; Perelman, 1960; Blinder, and Kirschenbaum, 1967).

Most of the papers published by various workers describing their experience in treating married couples in groups have shown a positive response to their experiment, but a few have had serious reservations (Blinder and Kirschenbaum, 1967). Blinder states that the therapy group obtains for its members a healthier marital equilibrium through correction of perceptual communicative errors, alleviation of reciprocal anxieties, analysis of discrepancies, and facilitation of intimacy. The patients' participation in the group process allows them to constructively examine the effects of their behavior and to experiment with alternatives.

Groups can be composed of couples with one therapist, or co-therapists can be used. There are advantages and disadvantages to each. In England, a single therapist for groups is usually the rule, while in America co-therapists are more frequently used. The single therapist is economical and avoids the transference problems between the co-therapists. The co-therapist approach, using a male and a female therapist, has marked advantages of increasing the types of responses from the patient couples, allowing supervision and support of one therapist for the other, and giving the opportunity for the patient couples to observe and learn from the therapist couple's interactions. This approach is not as economical and requires a good working relationship between the therapist couple.

James Jackson and Martin Grotjahn (1958a and 1958b) utilized combined individual and group therapy. When a patient was in group therapy and had reached a stalemate in the treatment due to a blocking marriage neurosis, the mate was brought into the group temporarily. The mate's presence was used to reactive the oedipal conflict, thus changing the blocked patient's transference neurosis to a workable transference so that interpretation became effective. A variation of this mix of group and couple is the placing of husband and wife together in a group of unmarried patients (Gottleib, 1960).

James Framo (1973), reporting on his experiences with over two hundred couples, believes that couples group therapy is the treatment of choice for marital problems.

Advantages

1. Couples in such a group come to realize that their marital difficulties are not unique.
2. Other couples' marriage struggles are used as models of what to avoid and how things can be worked out.
3. Unrealistic expectations of marriage and of mates are exposed to the reality testing of the group.
4. Transference and countertransference feelings are diluted.
5. Group process is used for therapeutic leverage.
6. The method is economical and time saving.

Disadvantages

1. Excessive group contagion of hopelessness.
2. An unusual mix of destructive, aggressive personalities within the group (excessive psychopathology).

Indications

1. Can be used routinely as a practical, efficacious form of marital therapy.
2. When other forms of marital therapy have reached an impasse and the leverage of the couples group can vitalize therapy.

Contraindications

1. Family secret.
2. Inability of one mate to work with a group.
3. When one mate is psychotic or verbally unrestrainedly destructive.

HISTORICAL INTERLUDE—GENERAL SYSTEMS THEORY
(1960's and 1970's)

During these years a new wave, general systems theory, seems to be sweeping into the field of family and marital therapy. Although many important contributors are leading the way, this approach still seems to be in a state of confusion. The confusion arises in part because of the lack of precision of language used by protagonists of this approach. One reads in the literature the use of Communication Theory as if it were different from general systems theory or at least interchangeable. By others, communication is referred to as one subset of G.S.T.—the way information is transmitted within the system. Also, information theory and communication theory, as well as cybernetics and the concepts of these disciplines, are used interchangeably. This lack of precision, leading to lack of clarity in transmitting information, will affect my presentation in the following paragraphs.

General systems theory, founded by Ludwig von Bertalanffy, postulates that organized complexities, or "systems," are the product of the dynamic interaction among their parts, rather than the sum of their absolute characteristics. Thus the whole is not simply the sum of its parts but an integrated entity (von Bertalanffy, 1974).

Although von Bertalanffy maintained that psychoanalytic theory was incompatible with his views, many current-day analytically oriented group and marital therapists consider the basic principles of systems theory to be compatible with their theoretical orientation. However, the issue of compatibility is still debated vehemently by others (Durkin, 1972). Durkin suggests that general systems theory may provide the much needed unifying trends for the expanding and conceptually fragmented field of group therapy. She concludes on the basis of evidence that the conceptual systems of psychoanalysis and general systems theory are harmonious in principle and that their differences will eventually prove to be complementary rather than contradictory.

General systems theory was greeted with great enthusiasm in psychiatry during the middle 1960's and seemed to have faltered for a while. This may have been caused by a number of factors. Psychiatry is traditionally concerned with the individual. It is harder to see the individual as a functioning system than to see groups or families as systems. Also the difficulty of conceptualizing both emotions and cognitions in systems terms proved to be a formidable task. In addition there was a fear that conceptualizing the individual in systems terms would be dehumanizing and mechanistic. Considerable work is being done now to remedy these defects with movement toward development of theoretical expansions that have more direct and applicable relevance to psychiatric theory and practice (Gray, 1973).

In the earlier section on conjoint therapy, reference was made to the work of Don D. Jackson and his group. At that time, he called his new method an operational approach. Since then it seems to have been placed within the framework of general systems theory. Among the important contributors to the literature associated with this approach are Gregory Bateson, Jay Haley, Lynn Hoffman, Paul Watzlawick, John Weakland, Richard Fisch, Salvador Minuchin, and Milton Erickson.

Gregory Bateson (Bateson, 1972) is the anthropologist in the Palo Alto research group of the mid-fifties which produced the "double-bind theory of schizophrenia." He influenced the shift of emphasis onto the family as a whole and to the transactions within it as they take place in the present. In the clinical setting the therapist watches the patterns of communication, the structure of their conversation, the form and sequence of transactions that take place. In Bateson's double-bind theory the schizophrenic's type of communication was an adaptation to a mother who put the child into a paradoxical bind by giving him mutually contradictory messages while forbidding the child to recognize or point out what she was doing. The solution to the double-bind is to point out what the other person is doing. Since the child must maintain the relationship, he sacrifices himself in order to maintain the pretense that the mother's contradictory messages make sense. Bateson's frame of reference was to think "ecologically" in terms of patterns and relationships rather than in linear fashion as one does, for example, in thinking in terms of cause and effect. The double-bind theory per se has not stood up completely to the test of time, but it has had tremendous influence in developing important strategies of psychotherapy and contributing greatly to the growth of general systems theory and its application to the practice of psychotherapy.

Jay Haley has had a great influence on the field of marital therapy with his application of the implications of double-bind theory (Haley, 1963a). He shows how every communication functions both as a report and as a command. As a command each communication can be seen as redefining the nature of the relationship one is having with the partner. Thus in every relationship, such as in marriage or in therapy, there is an ongoing implicit power struggle over who defines the nature of the relationship. All symptoms of "disturbance" are in this way looked at as strategies that control relationships that cannot be controlled by other means. All situations in which one person sets out to change another have in common the use of "benign" double-bind communications which make it impossible for the patient to re-create the kinds of relationships he has formed in the past. Haley applies these concepts to marriage therapy (Haley, 1963b) with the focus on the distressed marital relationship and symptom formation. The marriage is the patient and not the individuals involved in the marriage. (This approach to marital therapy often puts the therapist in a double bind. When the patient and the relationship are dealt with separately, there is set up a peculiar form of unintended dualism, for each person is more than that which is reflected of him in his marriage [Sager, 1966a]). Haley presents the presence of the therapist as the couple's acceptance of an authority figure, and their acceptance of a "complementary" relationship because the therapist is the authority and the "rights" of patient and therapist are not equal. This complementary situation becomes part of the process of working out relationships in which each partner attempts to use the third person who has entered their relationship. Haley states that marriage therapy offers a context in which a couple can learn alternative ways of behaving while being forced to abandon those past procedures which induced distress.

In a different application of the systems approach to marital process (Backus, 1975), an event of marital communication is conceived of as a cybernetic system composed of many parts and stages. "Couple communication is presented as a feedback loop based on congruent transmission and effective reception of personal and interpersonal information. Couple negotiation is viewed as a system in development. Connections between component subsystems are mapped along with

TECHNIQUES OF MARITAL THERAPY   135

the pathways of progression from one stage to the next. No subsystem is taken as final but is constantly reworked in relation to the system as a whole" (p. 201). Clinical application of this construct emphasizes growth, learning, and adaptation. Outmoded patterns are seen not so much as pathology but as previously learned patterns which are to be unlearned while new and more appropriate responses are adopted.

The literature of the field of "marriage counseling" has recently been emphasizing what it calls communications theory (Bolte, 1970). It is a part of general systems theory following much of the work of Haley. However, as so often happens, what seemed to be a relatively simple approach is developing greater depth and scope as clinical experience inevitably dictates (Miller, et al., 1975).

HISTORICAL INTERLUDE—BEHAVIOR THERAPY (1960's-1970's)

Behavior therapy could have been placed under the preceeding section of general systems theory. When behavior therapists state that at times a cognitive restructuring process may be necessary before lasting behavioral changes can be effected (Knox, 1971), the single classification is warranted. However, the cast of investigators is quite different. The father of behavior therapy is B. F. Skinner (1953). As with general systems theory, early proponents of behavior therapy took the position that it was incompatible with psychoanalysis and vice versa. Recently the literature has contained articles on the compatibility of psychoanalysis and behavior therapy and their simultaneous use (Birk and Birk, 1975). Whatever the future may bring, it is still true that coexistence, convergence, or conceptual integration has barely begun between behavior therapy and psychoanalysis. Birk and Birk (1975) state: "The insight-seeking methodology of psychoanalytic psychotherapy and the change-producing techniques of behavior therapy form a complementary system: the former seems to uncover the early developmental learning experiences that shaped the later maladaptive and overgeneralized emotional/cognitive/behavioral habits, thereby providing therapeutically powerful counterinstances to the patient's prevailing faulty world-view and self-evaluation" (p. 510).

Behavior approaches to marital problems specify the problems in concrete and observable terms, using empirical principles of learning in working toward therapeutic goals (Liberman, 1970). When marital therapy is successful, it is because the mates have changed their ways of dealing with each other. In behavioral terms the ways of dealing with each other are translated into consequences of behavior or contingencies of reinforcement. Instead of rewarding maladaptive behavior, the marital partners learn to give each other recognition and approval for desired behavior. In order to accomplish this, a diagnostic procedure is necessary that involves making a behavioral analysis of the problem. This procedure is explicitly and amply dealt with in the growing literature on behavior therapy in marital disorders (Liberman, 1970; Stuart, 1969; Carter and Thomas, 1973; Knox, 1971; Wieman et al., 1974; Carter and Thomas, 1973).

Having determined what has to be learned by the mates, the behavior therapist next attempts to implement the behavioral principles of reinforcement and modeling in the context of ongoing interpersonal interactions (Liberman, 1970).

Behavior therapy as applied to marital therapy often revolves around the strategy of *quid pro quo* negotiation. This method of mutual give and take has advantages and disadvantages. Typically: (1) the therapist helps the different parties identify the sources of their dissatisfaction and specify their requests for change; (2) the requested changes are stated in terms of the behavior of each party involved; and (3) reciprocal exchange is agreed upon and enacted by the negotiating couple, under the mediating influence of the therapist (Tsoi-Hoshmand, 1975).

The basis for this therapeutic approach is the definition of marital adjustment as the presence of mutually satisfying rewards or the equitable exchange of pleasing behaviors. The converse definition of marital maladjustment would be the presence of unfulfilled expectations of each other and of the relationship; or the consequence of negative interaction between the partners and the witholding from each other of the reinforcements they are capable of providing.

Advantages

1. *Quid pro quo* exchange often takes the form of rewarding events; its successful application could directly bring about the positive interaction desired by the partners.

2. By reinstating mutual satisfaction in problem areas, negative interpersonal events associated with witholding of rewards become unnecessary.

3. This problem solving strategy can replace frustrating modes of nonconstructive fighting over problems of dyadic living.

Disadvantages

1. Mates with unrealistic expectations for their partners or for the marriage relationship may not be able to negotiate for a satisfactory exchange.

2. Mates who doubt the other partner's commitment to the relationship, or have disqualified the partnership, will not be interested in *quid pro quo* negotiations.

3. When either or both mates insist on being infallible in attitude and refuse to abide by the rules of compromise, *quid pro quo* negotiation will not be acceptable.

4. Negotiated changes may not be successfully implemented or maintained without sufficient support; or when one or both mates are emotionally opposed to them or are unable to carry them out because of behavioral inadequacies.

Indications

1. Couples who engage in some form of negotiation similar to compromise by give-and-take.

2. When one partner always makes concessions and has unfulfilled needs.

3. When partners cannot come to an agreement on a rational basis.

Contraindications

1. When only one or neither mate has the available resources or the capacity to provide the other with what is pleasing.

2. When partners are not sufficiently committed to the relationship to invest in cooperative problem solving.

3. Mates who do not consider the marriage above absolute individual gains.

4. Mates who do not value the exchanged items or behaviors as sufficient rewards to maintain the negotiated reciprocity.

AUDIO-VISUAL TECHNIQUES IN MARITAL THERAPY, 1965

A recent technological development, videotaping (previously used for research and teaching), is now being utilized in therapy (Alger and Hogan, 1967; Alger, 1967, Alger and Hogan, 1969; Berger, 1970 and 1972). The technique involves the television recording of the first fifteen minutes of a conjoint marital session. The episodes recorded are then played back over a television monitor immediately so that all participants can stop the recording at any point to comment on their own behavior or that of others, their feeling reactions, and any discrepancies between the way they now appear and the way they remember actually feeling at the time of the original incident (Alger, 1967). For the first time in therapy, a tool is available that can provide the participants with objective data concerning behavior in therapy and that allows the review of the data immediately and as often as is desired.

Videotaping itself is not a method of therapy, but it can be an important means of enhancing the value of a particular therapeutic approach. Although more likely to be considered by therapists interested in field theory of behavior and communication theory in relation to therapy, it can be used therapeutically regardless of the therapist's theoretical orientation.

Advantages

1. Helpful in clarifying multiple and contradictory channels of communication.

2. Develops patient's depth of awareness of self more rapidly.

3. Enhances patient's motivation to remember this awareness and put the new awareness into practice without the common feeling of coercion.

4. Enhances awareness of underlying feelings in mates.

5. Reality of therapist not readily distorted by transference of patient.

Disadvantages

1. Technical problems with equipment causing poor visual or sound reproduction or breakdown of equipment.
2. Expense of equipment in private practice.
3. Preoccupation with the "media" rather than the "message."
4. Dehumanization of therapeutic relationship with anxious therapist.

Indications

1. Could be used for any couple at some time in their treatment.

Contraindications

1. Not to be used precipitously where the effect would be devastating (e.g., with an extremely overt, highly mannered bisexual mate or where excessive self-hate and suicidal impulses are tied up with body image, as in obesity); in short, when danger exists of bypassing the necessary defenses, with resulting emotional decompensation.

SUMMARY

A review of the literature on psychotherapy of marriage partners allows for the following observations. It is clear that the literature was originally predominantly psychoanalytic in nature. As such, the original therapeutic emphasis was on the development and the analysis of the transference neurosis. The classical psychoanalytic approach, and the concurrent, the consecutive, the collaborative, and the combined approaches maintained this emphasis. The main change in direction took place when a de-emphasis and avoidance of the transference neurosis became evident in the literature. The shift of emphasis took place in that the focus moved from the patient-therapist transferences to the transferences between the marriage partners to something entirely new. This new approach was to place the main emphasis on establishing new relationships between the partners in the family setting by experiences in the therapeutic situation and without emphasis on deeper understanding of transference reactions within the individual patient. This approach would recognize that changing the marital relationship produces some alteration of the personality of the individuals involved.

One of the several approaches in psychotherapy during the late 1950's and 1960's which illustrates the changing directions away from classical psychoanalysis was Roy Grinker's presentation of a transactional model for psychotherapy (Grinker, 1959). He describes avoidance of the development of a transference neurosis, but recognizes that he is still dealing with transference phenomena which he considers to be back-and-forth implicit communications between therapist and patient in which the present is colored by the past.

A further revolutionary development occurred with the work of the Palo Alto group and the growth into the general systems approach to psychotherapy. The field of marital therapy is still in ferment, as would be expected, since it is a reflection of the ferment present in the entire field of psychotherapy.

REFERENCES

Ackerman, N. W. (1958), *The Psychodynamics of Family Life*. New York: Basic Books.

Alger, I. (1967), Joint psychotherapy of marital problems. *Current Psychiatric Therapies*, Vol. 7. New York: Grune and Stratton.

Alger, I., and Hogan, P. (1967), The use of videotape recordings in conjoint marital therapy. *Amer. J. Psychiat.*, 123: 1425-1430.

Alger, I., and Hogan, P. (1969), Enduring effects of videotape playback experience on family and marital relations. *Amer. J. Orthopsychiat.*, 39: 86-98.

Backus, F. (1975), A systems approach to marital process. *Journal of Marriage and Family Counseling*, 1: 251-258.

Bateson, G. (1972), *Steps to an Ecology of Mind*. New York: Chandler.

Bateson, G., Jackson, D. D., Haley, J., and Weakland, J. H. (1956), Toward a theory of schizophrenia. *Behavioral Science*, 1: 251-264.

Berger, M. M., editor (1970), *Videotape Techniques in Psychiatric Training and Treatment*. New York: Brunner/Mazel.

Berger, M. M. (1972), The integrated use of videotape in the treatment of individuals, couples, families and groups in private practice. In *New Models for Group Therapy*, ed. H. S. Kaplan and B. J. Sadock. New York: E. P. Dutton.

Bion, W. R. (1961), *Experiences in Groups*. London: Tavistock Publications.

Birk, L., and Brinkley-Birk, A. W. (1975), Psychoanalysis and behavior therapy. *Amer. J. Psychiat.*, 31: 499-511.

Blinder, G., and Kirschenbaum, M. (1967), The technique of married couple group therapy. *Archives of General Psychiatry*, 17: 44-52.

Bolte, G. L. (1970), A communications approach to marital counseling. *Family Coordinator*, 19: 32-40.

Carter, R. and Thomas, E. (1973), Modification of problematical marital communication using corrective feedback and instruction. *Behavior Therapy*, 4: 100-109.

Cookerly, J. R. (1973), The outcome of the six major forms of marriage counseling compared: A pilot study. *Journal of Marriage and the Family*, 41: 608-611.

Dicks, H. V. (1952), Experiences with marital tensions in the psychological clinic. *British Journal of Medical Psychology*, 26: 181-196.

Dicks, H. V. (1963), Object relations theory and marital studies. *British Journal of Medical Psychology*, 36: 125-129.

Dicks, H. V. (1967), *Marital Tensions*. New York: Basic Books.

Drellich, M. G. (1968), Psychoanalysis of Marital Partners by Separate Analysts. In *The Marriage Relationship*, eds. S. Rosenbaum and I. Alger. New York: Basic Books, pp. 237-250.

Durkin, H. E. (1972), Analytic group therapy and general systems theory. In *Progress in Group and Family Therapy*, eds. C. J. Sager and H. S. Kaplan. New York: Brunner/Mazel, pp. 9-17.

Ezriel, H. (1950), A psychoanalytic approach to group treatment. *British Journal of Medical Psychology*, 23: 59-74.

Fairbairn, W. R. (1952), *Psychoanalytic Studies of the Personality*. London: Tavistock Publications.

Fitzgerald, R. V. (1973), *Conjoint Marital Therapy*. New York: Jason Aronson.

Framo, J. L. (1973), Marriage therapy in a couples group. *Seminars in Psychiatry*, 5: 207-217.

Gill, H., and Temperly, L. (1974), Time-limited marital treatment in a foursome. *British Journal of Medical Psychology*, 47: 153-161.

Giovacchini, P. L. (1965), Treatment of marital disharmonies: the classical approach. In *The Psychotherapies of Marital Disharmony*, ed. B. L. Greene. New York: Free Press, pp. 39-82.

Gottleib, S. B. (1960), Response of married couples included in a group of single patients. *International Journal of Group Psychotherapy*, 10: 143-159.

Gray, W. (1973), Emotional cognitive structures: a general systems theory of personality. *General Systems*, 18: 240.

Greene, B. L. (1970), *A Clinical Approach to Marital Problems*. Springfield, Ill.: Charles C Thomas.

Greene, B. L., Broadhurst, B. P., and Lustig, N. (1965), Treatment of marital disharmony. In *The Psychotherapies of Marital Disharmony*, ed. B. L. Greene. New York: The Free Press.

Grinker, R. (1959), A transactional model for psychotherapy. *Archives of General Psychiatry*, 1: 132-148.

Group for the Advancement of Psychiatry (1970), *The Field of Family Therapy*. Report No. 78: 525-644.

Haley, J. (1963a), *Strategies of Psychotherapy*. New York: Grune and Stratton.

Haley, J. (1963b), Marriage therapy. *Archives of General Psychiatry*, 8: 213-234.

Hollender, M. H. (1971), Selection of therapy for marital problems. In *Current Psychiatric Therapies*, ed. J. H. Masserman. New York: Grune and Stratton.

Jackson, D. D. (1957), The question of family homeostasis. *Psychiatric Quarterly Supplement*, 31: 79-90.

Jackson, D. D., and Weakland, J. H. (1961), Conjoint family therapy, *Psychiatry*, 24: 30-45.

Jackson, J., and Grotjahn, M. (1958a), The treatment of oral defenses by combined individual and group psychotherapy. *International Journal of Group Psychotherapy*, 8: 373.

Jackson, J., and Grotjahn, M. (1958b), The re-enactment of the marriage neurosis in group psychotherapy. *Journal of Nervous and Mental Diseases*, 127: 503-510.

Knox, D. (1971), *Marriage Happiness*. Champaign, Illinois: Research Press Co.

Kohl, R. N. (1962), Pathological reactions of marriage partners to improvement of patients. *Amer. J. Psychiat.*, 118: 1036-1041.

Kubie, L. S. (1956), Psychoanalysis and Marriage. In *Neurotic Interaction in Marriage*, ed. V. W. Eisenstein. New York: Basic Books, pp. 10-43.

Leichter, E. (1962), Group psychotherapy with married couples. *International Journal of Group Psychotherapy*, 12: 154-163.

Liberman, R. (1970), Behavioral approaches to family and couple therapy. *Amer. J. Orthopsychiat.*, 40: 106-118.

Martin, P. A., and Bird, H. W. (1953), An approach to the psychotherapy of mariage partners—the stereoscopic technique. *Psychiatry*, 16: 123-127.

Martin, P. A. (1971), Dynamic considerations of the hysterical psychosis. *Amer. J. Psychiat.*, 128: 745-748.

Miller, S., Corrales, R., and Wackman, D. B. (1975), Recent progress in understanding and facilitating marital communication. *The Family Coordinator*, 24: 143-152.

Mittelmann, B. (1944), Complementary neurotic reactions in intimate relationships. *Psychoanalytic Quarterly*, 13: 479-491.

Mittelmann, B. (1948), The concurrent analysis of married couples. *Psychoanalytic Quarterly*, 17: 182-197.

Mittelmann, B. (1956), Analysis of reciprocal neurotic patterns in family relationships. In *Neurotic Interaction in Marriage*, ed. V. W. Eisenstein. New York: Basic Books, pp. 81-100.

Neubeck, G. (1954), Factors affecting group therapy with married couples. *Marriage and Family Living*, 16: 216-220.

Oberndorf, C. P. (1934), *Folie à deux*. *Internat. J. Psychoanal*, 15: 14-24.

Oberndorf, P. (1938), Psychoanalysis of married couples. *Psychoanalytic Review*, 25: 453-475.

Olson, D. H. (1970), Marital and family therapy: integrative review and critique. *Journal of Marriage and the Family*, 32: 501-538.

Olson, D. H. (1975), A critical overview. In *Couples in Conflict*, eds. A. S. Gurman and D. G. Rice. New York: Jason Aronson, pp. 7-62.

Perelman, J. L. (1960), Problems encountered in psychotherapy of married couples. *International Journal of Group Psychotherapy*, 10: 136-142.

Reding, G. R. and Ennis, B. (1964), Treatment of the couple by a couple, Part I. *British Journal of Medical Psychology*, 37: 325.

Reding, G. R., Charles, L. A., and Hoffman, M. B. (1967), Treatment of the couple by a couple, Part II. *British Journal of Medical Psychology*, 40: 243.

Sager, C. J. (1966a), The development of marriage therapy: an historical review. *Amer. J. Orthopsychiat.*, 36: 458-467.

Sager, C. J. (1966b), The treatment of married couples. In *American Handbook of Psychiatry*, Vol. 2, ed. S. Arieti. New York: Basic Books, pp. 213-224.

Sager, C. J., et al. (1968), The married in treatment. *Archives of General Psychiatry*, 19: 205-217.

Satir, V. M. (1965), Conjoint marital therapy. In *The Psychotherapies of Marital Disharmony*, ed. B. L. Greene. New York: The Free Press.

Skinner, B. L. (1953), *Science and Human Behavior*. New York: Macmillan.

Spiegel, J. P. (1957), The resolution of role conflict within the family. *Psychiatry*, 20: 1-6.

Stewart, R. H., Peters, T. C., Marsh, S., and Peters, M. J. (1975), An object-relations approach to psychotherapy with marital couples, families, and children. *Family Process*, 14: 161-178.

Stuart, R. B. (1969), Operant-interpersonal treatment for marital discord. *Journal of Consulting and Clinical Psychology*, 33: 675-682.

Sullivan, H. S. (1953), *The Interpersonal Theory of Psychiatry*. New York: W. W. Norton.

Thomas, A. (1956), Simultaneous psychotherapy with marital partners. *Amer. J. Psychotherapy*, 10: 716-727.

Tsoi-Hoshmand, L. (1975), The limits of *quid pro quo* in couple therapy. *The Family Coordinator*, 24: 51-54.

von Bertalanffy, L. (1974), General system theory and psychiatry. In *American Handbook of Psychiatry*, 2nd. ed., Vol. 1, ed. S. Arieti. New York: Basic Books, pp. 1095-1117.

Watson, A. (1962), The conjoint psychotherapy of marriage partners. *Amer. J. Orthopsychiat.*, 33: 912-916.

Wieman, R. J., Shoulders, D. I., and Farr, J. H. (1974), Reciprocal reinforcement in marital therapy. *Journal of Behavior Therapy and Experimental Psychiatry*, 5: 291-295.

Wynne, L. C., Rycroff, I., Day, J., and Hirsch, S. (1958), Pseudomutuality in the family relations of schizophrenia. *Psychiatry*, 21: 205-220.

7

Selection of Therapy

WE ARE NOW READY to approach the complex problem of selection of therapy. The problem is so complex because the selection depends upon a blending of a variety of problems presented by a variety of combinations of individuals who make up the marriage, together with the often limited training and experience of the therapist. There is a marked difference between the ideal selection of one type of therapy from the wide assortment described in the last chapter and the practical choice determined by the balance between what can be offered by the therapist and what can be utilized by the marriage partners.

GUIDING PRINCIPLE OF SELECTION OF TREATMENT

The basic guiding principle is that the treatment should be fitted to the patient. Violations of this principle come from two opposite poles. One is the relative lack of didactic education and of formal supervised clinical experience in marital therapy in medical schools and training centers in the United States (Martin and Lief, 1973). Under these limitations the therapist may refer the couple elsewhere or try to fit the couple to the one form of psychotherapy with which

144

the therapist is comfortable. At the other extreme, the danger, as expressed by Hollender (1971), is that when enthusiasm is running high for the newest or most novel form of treatment, the available patient is fitted to that treatment.

Ideally, the initial diagnostic interviews, involving a detailed and thoughtful evaluation, are used as a basis for deciding first whether treatment is (1) required, (2) usable, and then (3) recommending the approach that is most likely to be helpful with the combination of the available therapists and the specific marital couple.

WHEN MARITAL THERAPY IS NOT RECOMMENDED

Therapy Is Not Needed

There are happy experiences where initial interviews reveal that no treatment is required and that to "begin treatment" with the first interchange between patient and therapist is, indeed, premature. These are usually cases of misinformation or examples of "tyranny of the ideal." They involve working marriages with good dovetailing of needs that do not fit mass media presentations of idealized marriage and sexual heroics.

Too Late for Therapy

There are other experiences when the couple is rejected for treatment because the marriage is beyond repair. Either mate may be looking for help to effect the separation or divorce with the minimum of hostilities.

Treatment Not Usable By Couple

Having determined that treatment is required, recommendation for treatment does not follow automatically. The reason for this statement is that many patients who are taken into treatment never enter into treatment. This is one of the reasons for the apparent relatively low percentage of good results with various forms of psychotherapy. If the surveys could distinguish between those patients who entered into treatment and those who merely attended, the percentage of success of psychotherapy would be much higher.

Often patients will state that presence in the therapeutic situation is proof of desire for treatment. This is often far from the truth. Many other factors determine their presence. One example is fear of the wrath or loss of the marriage partner if they did not attend. The most frequently encountered reason for the presence of a patient who does not want treatment is the patient's need to manipulate the therapist into accepting the patient's viewpoint as being valid despite all evidence as to its unrealistic and nonfunctioning aspects.

One of the common pictures in marital therapy where the diagnosis can be made of treatment being necessary but not usable is the wife who drags a resistant husband into the office so that the therapist can change him into what she knows he should be. This does not mean that the couple is discharged without treatment. It means the treatment contract that this type of wife wishes to impose is shown to be untenable. A workable therapeutic contract, pertinent to each couple, must be spelled out as clearly as possible before treatment starts. Otherwise treatment will fail unless a new contract is agreed upon at a later date. It is much easier to start with a workable contract than to change an established untenable therapeutic contract.

In the example given above it is best to make it clear as early as possible to the wife that each mate must take individual responsibility for change of self and of the relationship to the other mate. Manipulation of the mate is not the purpose of marital therapy. It can be pointed out that if the individual changes, there may or may not be a change in the relationship in response to the initiating change. If there is none, the initiator must then decide what to do. If there is a change, it may be in the direction desired or not. If it is as desired, there will be a happy marital equilibrium established. If not, further decisions face the individual mate.

Some mates (one or both), when confronted with such an approach, will decide against treatment. Others will decide for treatment consciously but remain as determined as ever to effect their own plan. This will be revealed as treatment develops and a simultaneous redefinition of both the marital and the treatment contract is necessary throughout the course of treatment.

Marital Enrichment Movement

There is currently developing in the United States a movement which could be called marital enrichment. It is in keeping with the general wave of encounter groups involving "healthy" individuals. This movement involves healthy marriages where there are no indications for treatment. A group of couples meet to increase the awareness of the positive aspects in a marital relationship (Clarke, 1970). These sessions help "normal" couples become more skilled in a type of dialogue that may be a forgotten or unlearned interpersonal art. With those couples where the diagnosis is that therapy is not needed, a suggestion for marital enrichment may be considered.

WHEN MARITAL THERAPY IS RECOMMENDED

Having decided that therapy is needed, the next question is: What type of treatment? Often it is possible to make such a determination without an exhaustive anamnesis. However, the more the therapist understands about each mate and about the marital relationship, the more likely he is to determine how best to proceed. Just as it is important to take a history before determining whether or not to recommend treatment, so too is it important to take a good history to determine what type of therapy to recommend. If we have decided that the patient wants therapy and can use it, the determining questions are: (1) What is it that the patient wants out of therapy and (2) is the patient capable of taking the primary responsibility to make it work? The two often do not coincide. As will be shown in the chapter on divorce, there is a type of problem in which the wife determines that if her husband does not change, she wants a divorce. When she gets the divorce, she is grief-stricken, having discovered that she was better able to maintain her emotional equilibrium with her husband as her support than when she was alone.

Sometimes it is not possible to make an accurate evaluation of what the individual is capable of effecting until after a moderate-to-long period of treatment. Thus reassessment and re-evaluation are a part of the treatment process.

Marital therapy is not limited to those people who suffer from psychosocial problems. Psychotic patients are not eliminated from consideration. The recent work of Greene et al. (1975) illustrates clearly that the presence of a psychiatric disorder may necessitate marital therapy to maintain homeostasis within the affected mate and even to prevent incipient attacks. Even with an underlying genetic factor in this type of disease and the availability of drug therapy to treat current and prevent future attacks, marital therapy is often indicated. Ludwig and Ables (1974), in reporting on the relationship between biological and behavioral variables, speculated "that mutual, nonverbal, subconscious biochemical communication between two intimate individuals can occur, not only altering their internal biological milieu but subtly affecting their outward behavior as well."

It has been found that effectiveness of lithium prophylaxis in treatment of bipolar patients is enhanced by accompanying marital therapy. Marital therapy in marriages marked by psychotic episodes in one mate is often productive and rewarding.

Marital therapy is a form of treatment that stands on its own; its limitations are determined more by the training and skill of the therapist than by a limitation to only psychosocial problems or problems of living. The marital therapy unit of husband, wife and one therapist "is group psychology for the smallest numerical group" (Dicks and Stevens, 1974), or family therapy for the smallest numerical group. Adding children to the basic unit may cause it to be called family therapy, or adding other couples may cause it to be called group therapy, but the therapeutic values of family or group therapy are present in their smallest unit called marital therapy. Some patients incapable of utilizing individual therapy benefit from marital therapy, even when there is no marital disharmony present and the other mate has no need for individual therapy.

SELECTION OF TREATMENT

The following outline of selection of therapy is a modification of the approach suggested by Hollender (1971) in his excellent review of the subject. The four categories presented here are not exclusive and at times may overlap.

With information from a careful evaluation, one of the four types of therapy can be recommended to the couple. In an earlier chapter,

I developed "normal" values for marriage. Contrasting the presenting marital disharmony with these normal values contributes to a formulation of treatment goals and the type of treatment to recommend to effect the necessary changes.

Person-Oriented Therapy

In this type of therapy one or both mates are in treatment. When only one mate is in treatment there is no communication between the therapist and the other mate. When both mates are in treatment there is also no communication between the therapists. The preceding chapter gives advantages and disadvantages as well as indications and contraindications for the various types of treatment that come under this category. Since the primary concern is for the individual, the outcome of the marriage will depend on the outcome of the individual therapies.

Marriage-Oriented Therapy

Here the primary emphasis is on resolving problems that interfere with a dovetailing of needs sufficient to make the marriage a harmonious one. This includes all types of therapy described in previous chapters, except where only one individual is in treatment and where husband and wife are in treatment with separate therapists and there is no communication between the therapist and the other mate or between the two therapists. Sometimes marriage-oriented therapy that fails in its original goal involves helping the mates toward a less destructive experience with divorce.

Combined Individual and Marriage-Oriented Therapy

In actual practice therapy is usually both person-oriented and marriage-oriented. In order to effect the dovetailing of needs, the person must take responsibility for individual change, for if there is first a change in the behavior that is lasting, it does have a secondary effect of an accompanying change in the person.

Sex Therapy

With the success of Masters and Johnson (1970) in the treatment of sexual dysfunction, the marital therapist is facing an identity crisis. When the evaluations show marital dysfunction mainly in the sexual area, or when previous individual or marital therapy for the couple has failed to resolve the sexual dysfunction, should the marital therapist refer the couple to sex therapists? Or should the marital therapist seek training in sexual therapy so that he can utilize these newer principles effectively and add them to his therapeutic armamentarium?

The success of the conjoint behavioral techniques has stimulated their use in the treatment of sexual dysfunction in the marital couple. This is in keeping with the experience of successes in conjoint marital therapy, since it can highlight the couples' interactional problems which are crucial vectors in undoing maladaptive mechanisms that have either initiated or maintained the dysfunction (Berman and Lief, 1975).

The use of these techniques (operant conditioning, contractual contingencies, and task assignments) in sex therapy is regarded as a form of desensitization and behavioral modification (Annon, 1974). The drawback in individuals not trained in marital therapy employing behavioral techniques is that they use them mechanically, in a nondiscriminatory fashion, without an awareness that their success is subject to all of the vicissitudes of the marital transactions. Sex therapy has been employed for a sufficient length of time now so that marital therapists are beginning to see couples who had been categorized as successes in their sexual therapy reverting back to the disharmony, including sexual difficulties, inherent in a disturbed interpersonal relationship. Berman and Lief (1975) state: "Sex therapy cannot be conducted separately from an examination of the couple's communication pattern and their wishes for and fears of intimacy and power. The relationship between sex therapy and marital therapy is a complex and as yet not clearly differentiated one. Sex therapy is not a subspecialty of marital therapy. The goal of marital therapy is the fostering of the growth of the two individuals by harnessing the forces within the marriage. The goal of sex therapy is to remove the dysfunctional symptom." The relationship of the marital discord to the sexual dysfunction can be categorized as follows: (1) Where the sexual dysfunction causes marital discord. Recommendation: Sex therapy. (2) Where the marital discord has impaired sexual functioning. Recommendation: Marital or Sexual Therapy. (3) Severe marital discord is present which precludes sex therapy. Recommendation: Marital Therapy.

It is my belief that sex therapy techniques will become integrated with marital and individual psychodynamics as is indicated in the work of Kaplan (1974). Training programs for comprehensive sex therapy within medical school settings are already beginning and will proliferate to meet the need for professionally qualified practitioners. Marital therapists are in a particularly advantageous position in participating in such training (Sadock, et al., 1975).

An as Yet Unproven Determinant in the Selection of Therapy

Clinical impressions have suggested to individual practitioners that one form of therapy is more advantageous than another. But there is a paucity of objective research to verify the greater value of one technique over another. Thus far it appears that the skill of the practitioner of the technique is the decisive factor. Reports in the literature show a trend away from concurrent to conjoint interviews and indicate that group methods are becoming more popular (Cookerly, 1973). A recent research study forces us to consider this aspect anew. Cookerly (1973) urges caution in interpreting the results of his study since it was only a pilot study and lacked the cautions and controls of a more rigorous research effort. Cookerly's study may be only a straw in the wind, but objective research is the direction which must be taken in marital therapy. His studies indicate that marked differences exist between various forms of marital therapy. This study suggests that different outcomes in marital therapy can be expected when different forms of marital therapy are used and that some forms are superior to others: "The rank ordering of the forms advances the concept that the conjoint interview and the conjoint group are the most effective forms, though conjoint interview may have disadvantages for those who divorce" (p. 610).

Concurrent interviews ranked as least or next to the least effective.

These findings are in keeping with clinical experience. That concurrent, though relatively ineffective, is the most common form of marriage therapy attests to the resistance to change in therapists uncovered in the survey of Martin and Lief (1973).

Individual interviewing wherein only one mate receives treatment is shown to be relatively poor for those remaining married, ranking equally low with concurrent therapy. However, it is quite helpul for those obtaining a healthy or compatible divorce.

Concurrent group, individual interview, and individual group were shown to be mixed and mediocre in their effectiveness. Generally, the group forms of marital therapy could be seen as doing a little better than the interview forms, especially for those obtaining divorces.

The tentative nature of this study dictates further research to determine whether the form of therapy should be a determining factor in the outcome of therapy. I would tentatively conclude from this study that, if the skill level of the various therapists are about the same, the type of therapy can have a significant effect upon the outcome. However, when there is a wide variation in experience and skill among the therapists, these factors can outweigh the specific technique.

Crisis-Oriented Marital Therapy

This section on crisis-oriented treatment is found under "Selection of Treatment" because the utilization of a specialized technique that has not yet been described here may be immediately necessary with the first interview, before any one of the already described forms of treatment can be selected. In addition to the already mentioned important contributions to marital therapy given to us by Bernard L. Greene and his colleagues is a technique called Transient Structured Distance (Greene et al., 1973). The following clinical vignette illustrates its use.

The call for treatment was a result of a crisis. The husband had severely beaten his wife and also physically abused her child from another marriage. He had lost the capacity to control himself in the face of the taunts, arguments, and complaints of his wife. It was a sado-masochistic relationship in which neither one could get along without the other, but the husband was provoked into violence with threats of shooting himself. (There was a shotgun in the house.) This pattern had repeated itself on several occasions during the preceding year, and earlier treatment with other therapists provided ineffectual. The technique chosen at the first interview, which was conjoint, was T.S.D. The husband was asked to enter a hospital voluntarily for further evaluation and treatment. There was to be no communication between husband and wife. Each mate was to be seen separately (concurrent therapy) until further decisions could be made by the therapist.

During the cooling-off period, the wife was seen both alone and with her child. An evaluation of each person and of their relationship was made. The issue of child abuse was an important one and, if it were to continue, would have to be reported to the authorities, with separation of the child for the child's protection. After a few weeks, conjoint sessions between husband and wife began. This was their only contact for two months. Only under these conditions was it possible to institute conjoint marital and family therapy without the threat of abuse, murder, or suicide. The use of this technique is also sometimes necessary after the form of treatment has been selected and treatment has been started.

Transient Structured Distance has three component parts. First it is a distancing maneuver for the mates that can allow them to re-establish, or establish for the first time, a constructive working relationship. Secondly, structuring is involved. This is an active intervention by the therapist in marriages that are locked into a spiraling kind of conflict that requires some kind of structuring to be made if human destructiveness is to be prevented. I would note here that in the structuring both a workable therapeutic contract and a workable marital contract are being established at the same time. The third aspect is the transient nature of the maneuver, one technique within the total treatment process. T.S.D. can also be used as a method of breaking a therapeutic impasse, as a cooling-off maneuver, or as a major method of management where this becomes the goal of treatment. It is also valuable as a diagnostic tool to uncover quickly some of the basic dynamics of a marital structure. Greene states that its limits are broad when used by a therapist with ingenuity. Its advantages are clearly defined in Greene's article (1973).

Crisis orientation pertaining to stages in the marital cycle, which has been referred to in the work of Berman and Lief (1975), as well as in the work of Greene, is not pertinent to this section on selection of therapy.

REFERENCES

Annon, J. S. (1974), *The Behavioral Treatment of Sexual Problems*. Honolulu: Kapiolani Health Services.

Berman, E. M., and Lief, H. I. (1975), Marital therapy from a psychiatric perspective: an overview. *Amer. J. Psychiat.*, 132: 583-592.

Clarke, C. (1970), Group procedures for increasing positive feedback between married partners. *The Family Coordinator*, 19: 324-328.

Cookerly, J. R. (1973), The outcome of the six major forms of marriage counseling compared: a pilot study. *Journal of Marriage and the Family*, 41: 608-611.

Dicks, H. V., and Stevens, H. (1974), Concepts of marital diagnosis and therapy as developed at the Tavistock Family Psychiatric Unit. In *Marital and Sexual Counseling in Medical Practice*, 2nd ed., eds. D. W. Abse, E. M. Nash, and L. M. R. Louden. New York: Harper and Row, pp. 139-154.

Greene, B. L., Lee, R. R., and Lustig, N. (1973), Transient structured distance as a maneuver in marital therapy. *The Family Coordinator*, 22: 15-22.

Greene, B. L., Lustig, N., and Lee, R. R. (1975), Treatment of marital disharmony where one spouse has a primary affective disorder. Presented at the Annual Meeting of the American Psychiatric Association, Anaheim, California.

Hollender, M. H. (1971), Selection of therapy for marital problems. In *Current Psychiatric Therapies*, ed. J. H. Masserman. New York: Grune and Stratton, pp. 119-128.

Kaplan, H. S. (1974), *The New Sex Therapy*. New York: Brunner/Mazel.

Ludwig, A. M., and Ables, M. F. (1974), Mania and marriage—the relationship between biological and behavioral variables. *Comprehensive Psychiatry*, 15: 411-421.

Masters, W. H. and Johnson, V. E. (1970), *Human Sexual Inadequacy*. Boston: Little, Brown.

Martin, P. A., and Lief, H. I. (1973), Resistances to innovations in psychiatric training as exemplified by marital therapy. In *Psychiatry: Education and Image*, ed. G. Usdin. New York: Brunner/Mazel, pp. 132-150.

Sadock, V. A., Sadock, B. J., and Kaplan, H. I. (1975), *Amer. J. Psychiat.*, 132: 858-860.

8

Psychotherapy of Marital Disharmony

GENERAL CONSIDERATIONS

IN THIS MANUAL I have attempted to present without bias the approach which I have developed for treating marital disharmony plus the innumerable other approaches developed by other therapists. During the past thirty years, I have experimented with the other approaches described in this book to the degree that I would have firsthand knowledge of what was reported upon in the burgeoning literature on marital therapy and thus be better able to understand techniques to which the other authors were referring. I also have been fortunate to be able to supervise the work of many other therapists at several training centers. My experiences with various forms of marital therapy are in keeping with the conclusions of the few controlled studies available and coincide with Marmor's position (Marmor, 1966): No one form of psychotherapy has proven better than others. By and large, mature, experienced therapists of different theoretical orientations achieve comparable results. Favorable psychotherapeutic results are more dependent upon the therapist's personal characteristics, empathic capacity, and clinical maturity than on his theoretical inclinations. In addition, as stated in the introductory chapter of this book, it has been my observation that approaches based on different theoretical orientations can be equally efficacious for the patient because there is a common denominator which underlies the diverse approaches. It is the complicated human being who is responding to the therapeutic process. We do not know why patients are attracted to different kinds of therapy. If we did, it would help explain why different techniques and approaches in psychotherapy can yield the same results.

However, based on these observations, my attitude has been to emphasize pluralism in the training of therapists. When flexible in approach, the therapist can offer that approach most likely to be utilized by the specific human being involved in that particular therapeutic encounter.

This is in keeping with the findings of Jerome Frank (Frank, 1975), who states that a review of the shared features of the psychotherapies suggests a somewhat unconventional approach to diagnosis. "Instead of trying to find the right clinical diagnosis, which seldom helps in selecting a suitable therapy, it might be more profitable to classify patients with respect to their relative predilection for or ability to respond to therapies which emphasize one of the shared features above another. . . . It would try to explore the expectations patients bring to therapy, their preferred type of success, their arousability and the like" (pp. 18-19). This approach puts the major responsibility on the therapist to be adaptable to the patient. Too often patients need to adapt to the therapist's approach. Those who are capable of this adaptation make the approach a successful one. Those who are not capable may drop out, never to succeed, or may move from one form of therapy to another that may prove more usable.

In the sections that follow, it is assumed that the therapist will bring that type of therapy in which he is trained to the special problems being spotlighted.

PSYCHOTHERAPY OF SPECIAL TREATMENT SITUATIONS

The "Love Sick" Wife and "Cold Sick" Husband

This clinical entity has been delineated in Chapter 2, both phenomenologically and psychodynamically.

Rarely can these women tolerate classical analysis. Their ego defect prevents it. Psychoanalysis involves frustration of the analysand and the development of insight instead of gratification of the patient's wishes. This set of conditions is too frustrating for these women to tolerate. They need and demand gratification so desperately that just as they cannot enter into a responsible marriage contract, they cannot hold to a responsible therapeutic contract. With them, the couch approach defeats its own purpose. They force parameters in the analysis. For example, they may not even be able to lie physically quiet on the couch—they may jump up, sit in a chair, turn over on their abdomens, and say "talk to me!" This has the meaning of "Feed me. Love me. Give me. Take care of me. Tell me I am great." The therapeutic goals must be limited. Any technical approach must bear in mind the tendency to regression in such patients.

Where there is a source of gratification possible other than from the mate, the prognosis is better. For example, it is helpful if the person is talented in some way, such as in the arts, music, law, and the like. Encouragement of the development and utilization of their talents is needed. A protective, giving environment encourages development of their talents. Also, tapping of latent ambitions can be decisive. Native creative capacities are the touchstone to displace the passive, dependent wishes. In those persons where success occurs the results are spectacular. In these cases, where insight therapy is possible, where structural changes can be achieved, the crucial therapeutic focus is as follows. First, the wife must be separated from her clinging relation to her husband. This can be achieved by the development of the transference neurosis through which the dependent attachment is shifted from the husband onto the therapist. This process allows for the exposure of the specific ego defect. They show an unquenchable thirst for narcissistic gratification. Any trivial offense or disappointment is experienced as a devastating blow to their self-esteem. This narcissistic injury is reacted to with a diffuse overwhelming response of instinctual aggressive energy that threatens dissolution of the ego. This danger forces an even more desperate clinging in the symbiotic position.

The therapist must thus assume a two pronged approach. One focus is on the ego. An effort must be made to develop a higher tolerance for narcissistic deprivation. The other point of emphasis is toward a diminution in the intensity of the infantile murderous rage.

Initially, the therapist must gratify a vital need in these women. The nature of this need was graphically described by one patient, who told her therapist, "We lack something—pectin—it doesn't jell. We search for some other person to supply this pectin." In other words, these women have extremely weak egos which are incapable of crystalizing independent personalities. Early in these marriages, the husband is able to supply the missing ego factor. However, as the need for a surrogate ego grows and finally becomes excessive, these husbands can no longer make up the deficit. It is for this reason that the therapist must initially meet the patient's need by becoming a surrogate ego early in the treatment. This replacement therapy, however, will obviously be no more lasting in its effectiveness than was the husband's early efforts. Thereafter the woman must undergo an intensive therapy aimed at the development of an adequate ego structure. One of the women who was successful described this process in herself as follows. "The essential something needed for a person to jell is pectin. Pectin is not giving a damn when other people criticize or try to deprecate you and not being terror-stricken that you are going to go crazy with fury."

The psychotherapeutic problem encountered results from the wife's resistance to efforts to distinguish her own difficulties from her complaints against the husband. With this type of patient, it is almost impossible for the therapist working alone with the wife to accomplish this disentanglement. Her constant use of the mechanism of denial and projection invariably leads to confusion. The wife actually enters into a life-and-death struggle to prevent the therapeutic separation from the husband, since the husband is often used to prevent the outbreak of a psychosis in the wife. In this connection, it should be noted that the unwary therapist may accept the unrealistic statements of these women without realizing that the wife's maneuvers are frantic ego defensive activities. In addition, even when fully aware of the wife's defensive maneuvers, he faces a dilemma. Confronted by the ever-present threat of psychotic break, the therapist is hard put to decide when to support and when to illuminate the defensive activities. His timing must be right. If too much support is given, the paranoid tendencies will be further entrenched and the husband will be antagonized. On the other hand, if interpretations are made prematurely, the wife may react with severe anxiety or further withdrawal from reality.

Because of therapeutic difficulties encountered with these women and because of their demands that their husbands be changed, the latter may be forced into treatment.

When we turn our attention to the psychotherapy of the "cold sick" husband, we must make a distinction between those who are truly as their wives describe them and those cases where the wives' descriptions have been projective identifications and the husbands are not only reliable, dependable persons but also warm and responsive. When the latter description turns out to be the reality, the therapeutic task is easy compared to the treatment of the truly cold, unloving husband. Conjoint psychotherapy best serves the purpose of helping the unchangingly dependent "love sick" wife. This technique helps to distinguish this type of wife from her husband in its quickly picking up her distortions of reality and her projections onto her husband. When the ideal of separation and individuation cannot be achieved, the husband can be utilized to achieve a less desirable but still workable goal. The prevention of a frank psychotic break is sometimes an immediate goal. With the insight achieved through the conjoint therapy, the husband can understand how he triggers his wife's responses. In the conjoint sessions, it is possible for the wife to understand that her husband does love her. Under such ideal circumstances, it is possible for her to at least change from a hostile complaining parasitic position to a pleasant, appreciative dependent position. The attainment of this goal brings peace to the family.

When the husband is helped through his treatment to know that his wife's demands are expressions of her sickness, he is able to be kinder and less cold in his defensive activities against her attacks. Armed with the understanding of his wife, the husband contributes greatly to the achievement of this intermediate goal by either (1) once more carrying the load for both partners through understanding or (2) even more desirable, encouraging his wife in the development of her native talents.

The very difficult therapeutic problem is when the husband is truly cold, distant, and unloving. In conjoint therapy the therapist is able to observe the relationship between the mates, as well as to experience the nature of the husband's transference to the therapist. The question becomes one of how to teach such a man to be able to love. Experience has shown that deprivation of warmth and love characterized the parental home. His hurt was sealed over with a wall of cold hate, in contrast to the hot anger of the wife. Though the hate is of comparatively low intensity, it is an unrelenting and unforgiving grudge against women. The wife can have explosive episodes and be over it and loving. The husband never forgets or forgives. Therapy is thus directed to uncovering the feelings of hurt and pain beneath the cold exterior. The breakthrough of the repressed tears and rage often presages a turning point of rediscovery of warmth, love, and a new experience of life. The wife may be surprised to discover that her husband does get hurt and how she did contribute to the coldness which characterized the mate.

Treatment of the sexual problems follows the understanding of such difficulties with this marriage pattern, as described in Chapter 3. Sexual therapy techniques have been found to be most effective in correcting the sexual dysfunctions of this type of marriage (Jacobs, 1974).

Before concluding this section the important role of countertransference must be mentioned (Bird and Martin, 1956). As described, these wives prove to be dependent, clinging persons who express a great need for help. They rapidly develop what appears to be a strong positive transference to their therapists. This tends to arouse in the therapist both sympathy for the hapless wife and antagonism to the allegedly unloving, unprotecting husband. For the inexperienced therapist and for the therapist who is steeped in the need to give "tender loving care" to all patients, this type of woman is a tender trap. In order for therapeutic success to be possible, such an initial countertransference to a helpless female must be eliminated without the loss of empathy or replacement by hostility when the trap is sprung and the psychiatrist discovers the futility of his efforts.

The husband's therapist is in danger of falling into a different trap. He may at first be frustrated at not being able to uncover evidences of illness in the husband. He may, in addition, be irritated because the husband displays little interest in his offer to be of help. As a result, the therapist may at the outset join the wife in denouncing the husband and concur in her opinion that the husband is a cold person. Therapists often need very much to be needed and cannot stand to treat patients who seem not to need them.

Over a long period of therapy, when the wife's impaired cognitive functioning prevents utilization of the countless insights recognized by her, therapists tend to react negatively as they become disillusioned. In contrast, with intact cognitive functions, the husband may become the "good" patient the therapist desires. Care must be taken for the patients' benefit that countertransference reactions do not cloud one's clinical judgment nor impede the therapeutic efforts.

The "In-Search-of-a-Mother" Pattern

In this pattern, as delineated in Chapter 2, we see the reverse of the "hysterical wife-compulsive husband" in that it is the husband who is in search of "love" from another woman and the wife who is considered to be cold and unloving. When the husband is unable to carry his responsibilities at work and is incapacitated by symptomatology or impending regression, he blames his wife and looks elsewhere for intimacy and love that will enable him to maintain his equilibrium. To the degree that he is able to get this through his "in-search-of-a-mother," he does not feel the need for treatment. When he is rejected by the other woman, his anxiety level forces him into treatment. The dependency needs are displaced onto the therapist and the transference neurosis that develops clarifies the psychodynamic problem. Reestablishment of his self-esteem through his work situation with minimizing his dependency upon a mother figure becomes a key factor in his therapeutic progress. Bringing the wife into therapy through one of the forms of conjoint therapy clarifies the unworkable marriage contract and allows for a mutually responsive contract to reestablish marital harmony. Any disturbance in the sexual sphere of functioning for this pattern, as described in Chapter 3, is remedied to allow for the dovetailing of needs that will establish a workable marriage. The premature ejaculation and primary orgasmic dysfunction respond well to Masters and Johnson type sexual therapy.

It is usually easier to succeed in working with those wives who maintain a cold obsessive defense and to bring about a response of love than it is to work with the husbands showing the same character structure and defenses of the preceding pattern.

The "Dependent-Dependent" Marriage

Psychotherapy of the double-dependent marriage pattern is probably the most difficult therapeutic task in marital therapy. In the two preceding patterns one marriage partner was not emotionally incapacitated and could be utilized to take a greater share of the responsibility for a workable marriage. The therapeutic task in this pattern is to enable at least one of the two mates to separate and individuate, and develop some of the capacities summarized on page 80: capacity for independence, for supportiveness to mate, and for love, lust, and sensuousness. This, of course, is especially true if there are children in the family. This group is particularly illuminating of the phenomenon of neurotic marital interaction and neurotic marital equilibrium. It is at first surprising to note that if one of the dependent mates begins to progress toward independence and assumption of work responsibilities that will make the family financially solvent, the other mate will attempt to sabotage the therapeutic efforts. The struggle by the unchanging mate to preserve the pathological marital equilibrium is based on a fear of loss of the developing partner.

Sexual problems are frequent in this type of marriage, as described in Chapter 3, and remedial efforts in this area contribute much to initial development of self-esteem, as well as to establishing a healthier marital equilibrium.

This pattern in particular gives warning to therapists to recognize the wide variations in patterns of functional marriages and to take care not to push the couple to an ideal chosen by the therapist. The therapeutic ear needs to be carefully tuned to that level of equilibrium that such couples are willing and able to establish.

The mates may respond to sexual therapy. However, when depression is present in one or both mates, it is contraindicated.

The Paranoid Marriage

Psychotherapy of the paranoid marriage proceeds with extreme caution based on the understanding that the marital system meets important psychological needs of both the husband and the wife. Treatment of the paranoid individual in the marriage proceeds from a recognition that conjugal relations induce in the patient a general feeling of inadequacy with which he or she copes by utilizing the defense mechanisms of denial, reaction formation, and projection, among others. These persons are extremely sensitive to narcissistic injury, and the caution and patience of the therapist involves sensitivity to the patient's panic responses to recognition and admission of inadequacies. Establishing a trusting, working relationship in therapy is a hazardous effort, since the therapist at first becomes invested with the paranoid ideation.

In marital therapy, the problem that may be encountered very early or even prior to the marriage (long before clear-cut paranoid features appear) is jealousy. The jealous mate notes all of the partner's actions, demands that conversation or contact be limited, expects complete compliance, and often receives initial compliance from the partner, who dislikes arguments. Initial peace is achieved at the price of growing resentment (Morgan, 1975). After this mechanism fails because of depression or explosion of the resentment, marital therapy may be sought.

Therapy must be undertaken with both partners. Fears, depression, and resentments are given opportunity for expression and relief. If treatment is begun early, so that too many narcissistic injuries have not already led to delusions or a desire for revenge, the therapist can help the mate to listen to the jealous individual both accurately and sensitively and with an awareness that his self-esteem and personal and sexual confidence are low and need to be promoted. The self-esteem of the partner is also low from participating in the subjugation situation. Analysis of transactions can help to alleviate the symptoms if the therapist is accepted by both members of the partnership. The paranoid patient is hypervigilant during the interviews. The therapist must attempt to help the mate to be aware of how the words and actions are being carefully observed. The therapist is faced with the difficult task of evaluating whether accusations of infidelity are real, suspected, or delusional. I have found that in some obviously delusional paranoid mates, the suspected infidelity was real. In the therapy, suspicions are modulated by reality contact, fluid delusions can be modified, though perhaps only temporarily and only after an impressive marshaling of counterevidence; and fixed delusions are virtually uninfluenced by negative experiences (Abroms et al., 1966).

Though sexual problems abound, as delineated in Chapter 3, early sex therapy is contraindicated in this type of marital pattern. Indiscriminate or premature utilization of sex therapy prior to long-term psychotherapy may precipitate adverse reactions, including psychotic episodes in some partners (Kaplan and Kohl, 1972).

Accusations of infidelity in cases of conjugal paranoia must be differentiated from pathological jealousy of weak, insecure, and possessive persons (Revitch, 1960). The latter are treatable; the former are not. Revitch recommends separation for conjugal paranoia since the paranoid spouse cannot establish a therapeutic relationship. Conjoint interviews are necessary to avoid the danger of misdiagnosing the healthy spouse as paranoiac or mentally ill.

PSYCHOPHARMACOLOGICAL ASPECTS OF MARITAL THERAPY

Extensive experience has shown that psychotherapy is not enough to stabilize some psychotic conditions and psychoneurotic conditions involving severe anxiety. Drug therapy is either the treatment of choice in these conditions or a necessary adjunct. In addition, these drugs need careful supervision since they possess dangers of serious side effects.

The work of Bernard Greene and his associates in doing marital therapy with primary affective disorders best illustrates the principle that marital therapy deals with much more serious problems than is recognized even by experts in psychotherapy (Greene et al., 1975). It is in marked contrast to uncomprehending statements which relegate marital therapy to an unimportant superficial type of therapy. The ever-present threat of serious psychotic episodes (manic or depressive), or of serious suicide attempts, during the course of marital therapy necessitates well-trained therapists with access to hospitalization of patients. In addition, because of the marked variability of symptoms in primary affective disorders, there is a need for knowledge of a variety of drugs (tricyclics, MAO inhibitors, lithium carbonate, haloperidol, or phenothiazine derivatives). All these medications need careful and regular monitoring.

Greene, using general systems theory as a backdrop, explains the treatment of primary affective disorders by marital therapy as follows: "As indicated earlier, it is because of the open nature of the boundaries between the GST systems, that we see the ability of each system to affect processes taking place in the others and consequently affecting human behavior. . . . One of the special features of a PAD is that his boundaries are even more open than usual during a hypomanic or manic episode. One way to conceive of this is to see the PAD as biochemically primed, and supersensitive to family transactions and environmental influences" (Greene et al., 1975a).

Greene has developed an innovative approach to treatment of primary affective disorders. Counseling with a marriage where one spouse has such a disorder can be difficult and unrewarding. These marriages are characterized by "intermittent incompatibility" where a basic pattern of intimacy and cooperation is periodically interrupted by sudden and unexpected periods of intense conflicts, triggered by mood swings of the affected spouse. This marital conflict is then presented to the therapist as "uproar." Greene has stopped using the conjoint approach with such patients. As long as the therapist retains the conjoint approach, the conflict remains impervious to traditional techniques. The affected mate is generally already undergoing psychiatric treatment, e.g., chemotherapy. Hence, after noting serendipitously a relatively low divorce rate for such cases, Bernard Greene developed a management approach which focused attention on the role of the unaffected spouse. Essentially the treatment is to help this spouse accept that his or her mate has a recurrent biochemical condition. A complete history is needed to trace the disorder generationally both backwards and forwards. This history is not only of diagnostic importance but also useful to convince the mate of his condition, and generally leads to a positive shift in the marital interaction. In many cases the mate's new-found ability to maintain distance during an episode leads to a marked reduction in destructive interaction.

The same principle of combining drug therapy and marital therapy for schizophrenic patients has proven efficacious as a general systems theory technique.

The Use of Dreams in Marital Therapy

The value of the use of dreams in conjoint marital therapy is best illustrated by clinical material.

Mr. and Mrs. B were in marital therapy because of loss of impulse control in the husband, with physical battering of his wife and depression in the wife. Interest in dreams as part of the therapy had been indicated since the initial diagnostic interviews. He had come to a crucial point in therapy. The violence had subsided, the wife was still depressed and the husband insisted everything was well, and treatment should stop. Based on the strength of the transference relationship, the wife resisted his demand.

The husband was visibly shaken at the beginning of the hour. He reported having nightmares during the night. "We were walking through this cornfield. I was with a girl—a foreign girl. There was a grave in front of us—terrifying. I held out my hand. She went into a trance and was able to walk over the grave. We were in a room on the bottom floor of a dormitory. Impending disaster. I hide her in a closet but know that she will be found. I bolt the door but the angry hostile mob breaks through."

The wife, appearing wan and lifeless, reported her own "nightmare." She is looking at a peculiar figure. It is a fish hooked through the mouth that has small arms and legs somewhat like a human being. She is terrified. Working over several sessions with these two dreams, which confirmed his ability to control her by utilizing her fear of violence, allowed for the uncovering of (1) the marriage contract—conscious and unconscious, (2) the marriage pattern, (3) the therapeutic contract—or lack of one and (4) the transference neuroses of both partners. The importance of the use of the dreams in this manner was not the knowledge gained by the therapist through this material. Most of it had already been understood. The importance of the matched dreams was that they presaged a change in the marital relationship. The husband began to give up his control over his wife. It turned out that he really loved her but had been afraid of domination by a woman as he had dominated her. Her dream, illustrating her low self-esteem (a subhuman identity), became a turning point in her therapy, with increasing freedom from fear and depression.

Despite all initial predictions to the contrary, their marital therapy was successful.

Greene (1970), using dreams extensively in triadic sessions, states that they provide verification and clarity of understanding of the marital transactions and also of the various levels of transference phenomena. Dreams offer a point of departure for communication.

Martin Goldberg (1974) reports on how he uses dreams in conjoint marital therapy. They can be used where a strong therapeutic working alliance exists. He illustrates how the therapist structures their discussion in such a way as to encourage positive use of dream material such as the recall of childhood memories and the mutual discussion of areas of deep feeling. Use of this technique enhances communication and closeness between a couple.

Using the Marital Contract as a Therapeutic Technique

In Chapter 4, the intricacies of the marital contract were described. In the preceding section of this chapter an illustration was given of a use of dreams which leads to clarification of the marriage contract. I will use the same material to illustrate the use of the marriage contract as a therapeutic technique.

In the above described marriage the conscious contract was that the husband would protect his wife and bring excitement and interesting activities into her drab life. In return she would be appreciative and love him. On an unconscious level, she felt inhuman, like a half-dead fish. She needed him to make her feel alive and human. On an unconscious level, he felt inferior to other men and fearful of losing her to them. His defense was to terrorize her into unthinking compliance.

Having them write a conscious contract that was agreeable to both was the relatively easy portion. The difficult portion was rewriting the unconscious contract. The first step, obviously, was to make them conscious of the contract. With a good working therapeutic relationship, each mate's knowledge of the other's underlying needs and fears leads to a knowledge that each is frightened and needy. The defenses of violence or depression (in this example) are recognized as defenses. Repeated recognition and working through of the same problems without narcissistic injuries and hostile reactions allows for structural changes that are reinforced through the therapeutic approach. This is an exciting approach only possible with highly motivated, creative marriage partners.

USE OF THE "NORMAL" VALUE SYSTEM AS THERAPY OF MARITAL DISHARMONY

Chapters 2 and 3 were utilized to develop normal values for marriage. The normal value system of psychotherapy does not attempt to develop an ideal marriage. It attempts to develop enough of the six capacities listed (independence, supportiveness, acceptance of support, lust, sensuousness, and love) in each mate to establish, through dovetailing of needs, a functioning marriage. This, together with utilization of the marriage contract as described in preceding sections, forms a compact therapeutic approach.

REFERENCES

Abroms, G. M., Taintor, Z. C., and Lhamon, W. T. (1966), Percept assimilation and paranoid severity. *Archives of General Psychiatry*, 14: 491-496.

Bird, H. W., and Martin, P. A. (1956), Countertransference in psychotherapy of marriage partners. *Psychiatry*, 19: 353-360.

Frank, J. D. (1975), An overview of psychotherapy. In *Overview of the Psychotherapies*, ed. G. Usdin. New York: Brunner/Mazel, pp. 3-21.

Goldberg, M. (1974), The use of dreams in conjoint marital therapy. *Journal of Sex and Marital Therapy*, 1, 1: 78-81.

Greene, B. L. (1970), *A Clinical Approach to Marital Problems*. Springfield, Ill.: Charles C Thomas, p. 370.

Greene, B. L., Lee, R. R., and Lustig, N. (1975), Treatment of marital disharmony where one spouse has a primary affective disorder. *Journal of Marriage and Family Counseling*, 1: 82-101.

Greene, B. L., Lustig, N., and Lee, R. R. (1975a), Treatment of marital disharmony where one spouse has a primary affective disorder, III. General systems theory technique. Presented at Annual Meeting of American Psychiatric Association, May, 1975, Anaheim, California.

Jacobs, L. I. (1974), Sexual problems and personalities in four types of marriage. *Medical Aspects of Human Sexuality*, 8, 3: 160-181.

Kaplan, H., and Kohl, R. (1972), The possibility of adverse reaction to rapid treatment of sexual problems. *Psychosomatics*, 13: 185-190.

Marmor, J. (1966), The nature of the psychotherapeutic process. In *Psychoneurosis and Schizophrenia*, ed. G. Usdin. Philadelphia: J. B. Lippincott Co.

Morgan, D. H. (1975), Psychotherapy of jealousy. *Psychother. Psychosom.*, 25: 43-47.

Revitch, E. (1960), Diagnosis and disposition of paranoid marital partner. *Diseases of the Nervous System*, 21, 2: 20.

9

Divorce and Changing Marital Styles

THE IMPORTANCE OF VALUE SYSTEMS

I HAVE PLACED these different topics in the same chapter because therapy in these situations is so intimately involved with value systems. They involve the current values of the society, the values of the patients, and the values of the therapist more so than any of the previous subjects covered in this book.

Hollender (1959) succinctly states the issues that therapists must face. The therapist who does marriage-focused therapy must decide what will be good or bad for the marriage. When he functions to preserve a marriage he should recognize that he is an agent (or at least a representative) of society and that he is espousing its value system. The therapist is, of course, free to take any position he wishes, but he should be explicit about his stand both to himself and to his patients.

The problem of values and biases is accentuated when there are children. The therapist may feel that marriages should be held together for the sake of the children. The bias may be on behalf of the nuclear family. We will return to this bias in the second section of this chapter, which will deal with nontraditional family forms. Again, the therapist is free to elect this position, but he must recognize that

169

it is a value judgment, even if it is held by the majority of people in our society.

In a recent book on the divorced in America, Joseph Epstein (1974) expresses his advocacy of The Dream of Family which is shattered and often turned into a terrible nightmare by divorce. His advocacy of the family is based on the family being a unique situation in which one lives for something greater than oneself and a setting in which relationships are determined by considerations other than bargaining, responsibility or even decency. One does things for the others because they *are* one's family. He believes that only those who have lived it know the immense advantage it can be in an otherwise unconcerned world.

Epstein's emphasis on the family will also pertain to the "beyond monogamy" portions of this chapter.

The therapist has great difficulty in avoiding being sucked into cultural traps and reflecting current value systems at any point in the bell-shaped curve of values. For example, Epstein describes a currently competing dream—The Dream of the Self. He claims that our culture is increasingly coming to be dominated by ideas taken from psychotherapy. He describes it as a theme of: to thine own self be not merely true but to thine own interests give absolute primacy. "One's first responsibility is to one's self" is the slogan of the current revolution in America.

I think he gives psychotherapy too much credit. The rising divorce rate is a social phenomenon and is principally a reaction to the increased expectations and demands for autonomy and experience collection common to the 1960's (Berman and Lief, 1975).

What has happened through the decades is that psychotherapy styles and fashions have changed with the changes in the culture. The danger of the therapist following the current cultural changes is one of transmitting the values of separation and individuation, freedom and independence, to his patients indiscriminately, with disastrous results for some patients.

The danger of the therapist's doing harm is strongly underscored by Carl Whitaker and Milton Miller (1969). They suggest that in circumstances where divorce impends, the ordinary and customary styles of reacting to an appeal for help characteristic of general psychiatric practice may be inappropriate, ineffectual, or at worst, substantially detrimental. They state that accepting in therapy one member of a troubled couple should be viewed by the therapist as very possibly a step toward *preventing* a reconciliation. For many couples on the verge of divorce, the therapist becomes an alternate mate, no matter how scrupulous his efforts to avoid it. The therapist should be aware that he may be intervening and changing a process which, when nature takes its course, will heal.

Whitaker and Miller often find it necessary to remind themselves that as therapists they are in no position to offer a real substitute relationship for the mate who will be disappearing. This may be especially relevant if the therapist is comfortably married. Such a person is rarely able to anticipate or appreciate the loneliness, the despair, and the tedium in the life of a divorced person.

Whitaker and Miller believe that a provocation for divorce may constitute simultaneously a possibility for a heightening of engagement in a marriage that has grown stagnant—clearly a turning point. When the therapist enters into this situation and sees only one mate, he can, knowingly or not, be the leverage toward divorce. Their warnings would lead to a conclusion not to see one mate alone. Conjoint therapy, if any, would be indicated if the therapist has such a strong bias against divorce.

The problem then for the therapist is whether the goal is to preserve the marriage or to approach the presenting problems without regard for their effects on the marriage.

Clinical Material on Divorce

It is my clinical observation that most of my patients who talked seriously about divorce have not gotten divorces. This, of course, does not mean that psychotherapy resolves most marital problems. More pertinent is that many psychiatric patients are people who are anxiety ridden about separation, individuation, and both internal and external change. No matter how much they may complain about their marital partners, no matter how much the interpersonal bond is based on mutual hatred, they resist dissolving the relationship. These patients have never become separate individuals. They are symbiotically attached people who are terrified of being alone, of being individuals in their own right. They are unable to problem solve within the marriage, nor are they capable of leaving the marriage and problem solving free of the torturing mate. They have low self-esteem and accept being treated without respect by their mates rather than being alone.

These experiences recall another clinical entity reported in the literature involving divorce initiated by a certain type of woman patient. The note of warning is to the male therapist. These women involved in a positive transference to the male therapist blame their unhappiness or symptoms on being married to their husbands. The therapist may not clearly delineate that they are not making creative changes within themselves and are using the interpersonal conflicts to deny the need for inner change. The unwary therapist may even agree with them. An underlying fantasy that the therapist will take the husband's place is not explored and is not exploded. When the woman gets her divorce and the therapist does not replace the husband, the woman's lack of individuation, her lack of change through treatment, is exposed and she suffers anxiety and depression. The therapist may be considered by her to be at fault. Such women were better off remaining in the pathological equilibrium of the marriage than being alone on their own.

Another important factor in divorce to be considered by therapists is depression. Research studies on depression and marital turmoil show that 90 percent of divorced probands who had prior episodes of depression were depressed at the time of their marital separation or divorce (Briscoe and Smith, 1973). In fact, divorced depressives represent a more clearly defined group of persons with a depressive diathesis than do bereaved depressives. The studies conclude that depressions associated with divorce, unlike the depressions of bereavement that are the result of the death of a spouse, can be the cause of the marital turmoil as well as the result of the marital turmoil, or more complexly, both the cause and the result.

A clinician can anticipate that persons who have had depressive disease prior to any marital problem will have an episode of depression associated with their marital breakdowns. The research of Briscoe and Smith (1973) further supports the clinician who, regardless of the temporal relationship of the onset of a depression to marital turmoil, treats the depression, which could be a causative factor and not simply the result of the marital problems.

This material leads naturally to the problem of countertransference in the treatment of marital problems, especially where divorce is being considered. The therapist must be careful to avoid the natural tendency to side with the patient against the unknown mate. The therapist must be particularly aware of how often his patient uses mechanisms of denial, distortion, withholding of information, and even conscious lying to the therapist. Particularly, he must be aware of the frequency of projective identification in the production of such patients. What the patient is claiming to be actions, feelings, dynamics, or defenses of the mate is really what the patient is doing while camouflaging it by this mechanism.

These problems are minimized by using conjoint marital therapy. When the marital couple is seen at the same time both the confusing tactics of an individual patient and the countertransference complications of the therapist are minimized. However, this does not mean that conjoint therapy is the best therapy for all marriage problems. The issue of divorce particularly necessitates the capacity to provide that type of marital therapy which is best for a specific couple. As first presented in Chapter 5, results of the several types of marital therapy indicate that different forms of marital therapy tend to produce different outcomes (Cookerly, 1973). In general, conjoint forms are superior to others. The conjoint interview ranked first for the total population studied and for those remaining married, but was sixth or last for those obtaining divorces. The individual interview was third and fourth for the total number of subjects, fifth and sixth for the married group and second for the divorced subjects.

So if divorce is not considered with horror, or if it is even considered as indicated in some marriages, these findings can be used clinically. For example, a young woman, married four years, with no children, came to see me because she was unhappy in her marriage. She stated that she had married at sixteen to get out of her disturbed home and to get away from her difficult father. Immediately after her wedding she knew she had made a mistake. She was unhappy because she was unable to talk with her husband. He had a difficulty in understanding feelings—his own or others. He had difficulty in expressing himself. In contrast, she enjoyed talking with people, she enjoyed interacting with people. She was particularly careful to point out that her husband was a good man. He did not mean to make her unhappy. He did love her, he did want her, and did try to make her happy in his way. He simply did not know what she meant or what she wanted of him when she expressed her needs. She could not get through to him. He loved to watch sports and television. She tried but could not enjoy these things with him. She enjoyed music, art, and people. With no blame on either one, with no ill intent on either person's part, they were a mismatch. He couldn't give what she wanted. She couldn't enjoy what he did and couldn't give him what he wanted: acceptance of him as he was. The reason she couldn't do this for him, though she tried for four years, was that it meant giving up her self, her uniqueness, her identity. To live with him was to give up her self and to live with tears for what she was losing in life, to mourn her loss with a chronic depression. She did not want to do this.

The picture I have painted is not uncommon. It was clear that the wife would have to make a decision but might not be able to do this easily. I asked her if she wished to continue to come alone to explore her feelings further or to bring her husband with her to work together on their problems of lack of communication and lack of intimacy. She said she knew she could not stand to live with her husband as he was. If he remained the same she had to leave. She had a nice home and did not want to give it up but was prepared to do so.

She had just received a job promotion and was able to support herself and live in an apartment with a friend. She asked if her husband could change. I stated I did not know if he could change. I did know it was a difficult and time-consuming task. I would be willing to see him, if she wished, and further evaluate them. She stated that she was in a quandary. If he wasn't going to change, she did not want to lose further years while efforts were being made. I stated that I appreciated how she felt but only she could make the decision. If she wanted a divorce, individual therapy was better suited. If she wanted to maintain the marriage, conjoint therapy was better. She was nonplussed at first, but quickly came up with a compromise solution. Could she bring her husband and then if she saw he could not make the change, she would decide to leave without feeling guilty? I accepted her solution.

When her husband came with her, he confirmed the picture she had presented. He had the same difficulty in communication with other people as he did with his wife. His family history contained the same problem. After several sessions the wife called a halt. She no longer wished to remain in the marriage. She wanted to continue in individual therapy. The husband accepted her verdict and did not want individual therapy to change his problem or to get her back. He did learn that if he were to remarry he would do better with a woman who was like him and who could accept him as he was. The wife in this situation was clear in her knowledge of what she wanted in a man to dovetail with her needs.

Before I move to the positive, creative aspects of divorce, I want to emphasize once again the negative vicissitudes of breaking a marriage relationship, even a pathological one. Study of severely disturbed marriages confirms that there is a dovetailing of needs in these marriages, albeit a pathological dovetailing that keeps the pair stuck together with pain as the hinges grate against one another. To many people, even these mutual pain patterns are preferable to being alone —on one's own.

By this time I have case studies covering twenty years—which allows for a perspective not available in our reports published in the early years. It is surprising how different a case looks when reviewed ten to fifteen years later. One typical example from a group of similar cases involves a couple referred because the wife experienced psychotic-like panic reactions while hospitalized for unrelated surgery. After the wife entered psychotherapy it became clear that a severe marital problem was present. The husband was referred for individual therapy with use of the Collaborative Approach. At first the husband, successful in his work and presenting no symptoms, denied his wife's accusations about his cruelty to her and appeared to be the so-called "normal" American male. He quickly refused further treatment and his wife continued in her individual therapy. Her therapy was a difficult prolonged experience as she attempted to sever her pathological dependency upon her husband. She returned to college and began developing a career of her own despite her panic states.

As the years went by, the husband's previous drinking worsened and his suspicious tendencies developed into paranoid thinking. The more the wife changed and became independent, the more the husband decompensated. Despite her terrors the wife was forced to leave when the husband became psysically, as well as verbally, abusive. Divorce proceedings were initiated, separation effected, and the wife's psychotherapy successfully terminated.

Following this period the husband became openly psychotic, necessitating hospitalization. The wife continued in her career preparations at school. It appeared as if she had been vindicated and was fortunate to be free of her sick husband.

At this time I received a phone call from her asking for an appointment. She was having panic attacks again which threatened her work and her independence. She claimed to have no inkling as to why this was occurring. She did remember a nightmare. In it, her ex-husband was breaking her door down and was going to attack her.

Analysis of this manifest content revealed the true meaning of the dream. She was so terrified of being alone and becoming psychotic with terror that she was considering returning to her psychotic ex-husband, who wanted her back, even though she was terrified of him. The old symptoms and style had returned with the pressures of being self-supporting.

She couldn't believe that her old pattern and style had returned and was aghast that she would consider the old pathological solution again. She continued on her lonely but healthy way. Her husband remarried. Her last report was that she received a phone call from his new wife who tearfully reported that the husband was drunk, psychotic, and beating her up and asked the former patient what to do.

This history illustrates how people cling to old patterns of response and that change can be experienced as more terrifying than the most horrible old style of operating. Divorce, being self-supporting, and living alone are examples of such terrifying changes.

Another lengthy history illustrates how divorce must be understood in terms of the character structure of the individuals involved. Mr.

C entered therapy for panic attacks apparently associated with business pressures. He went from one business partner to another, never on his own and always complaining about being taken advantage of by the previous partner. He was not only very ambitious but, in hypomanic states, acquisitive of a wide variety of expensive items. In such states, he could never say no to his wants. At other times he would have depressive episodes in which he was aghast at his previous unrealistic activities. Through all these years, he leaned heavily on his wife. Whenever he was in need, she took care of him and mothered him through his panic or depressive episodes. For many years he spoke highly of her and talked of what a great marriage they had.

In another of his hypomanic episodes he found a younger, prettier girl with whom he fell madly in love. Like everything else before, he had to have her. He began complaining about his wife, left home, and started divorce proceedings. Now came the bind; through all the years of treatment he had not changed. He still could not say no to himself and his immediate wants. The divorce proceeded because he was unable to change, to accept the limitations of reality. But the therapy had succeeded to the degree where he recognized his pattern and he realized that after he had lost his wife and children he might tire of his new girlfriend as he had of previous possessions and find that he had lost everything. He wanted his family back. But he had gone too far. His wife wanted out and wanted no part of him. The divorce proceeded. His future of recurrent depressive responses was determined by his inability to change in the marriage. Thus lack of change not only contributes to the patient remaining in an unhappy marriage but also can cause a patient to seek a divorce.

It behooves the marital therapist to consider both marital separation and divorce as a life crisis. Psychological dysfunction, drug overuse, work and social dysfunction are observable areas of disturbance following the first serious mention of divorce, actual separation, filing for divorce, and obtaining the final decree. Suicide potential is greater during each of these periods of crisis.

Psychotherapy during the process of divorce is problematical. Even if they have received previous therapy, people are mostly bitter and revengeful during this period. There is a tendency to regress to primitive expressions of greed, vengeance, pettiness. There seems no limit to the hurt people will inflict on one another. Rarely are mates mutually decided to end the marital relationship on mutually agreeable terms. Either one has decided to end and the other has not or both have had enough and are fighting over money, custody, visitation— intensely personal areas (Felder, 1971).

Psychotherapy during this period tends to become stagnant. The person's attention is focused on external reality, on what is experienced as a fight for self-preservation in a war against a bitter enemy. The focus on an inner change often pales in comparison.

During this period therapists need to be especially careful not to allow themselves to get sucked into the divorce proceedings themselves. Divorce lawyers are experts in the field of not only protecting their clients' rights but getting the best possible settlement the law will allow, without concern for fair or not fair, right or wrong, justice or injustice. Therapists testifying in such situations are often made to look pompous and foolish by experienced lawyers. Therapists naturally tend to be overprotective of their patients, which is easily picked up by lawyers and turned against them. The problems of confidentiality and privileged communications become serious under these conditions. Even court-appointed therapists have difficulty in maintaining impartiality and dignity under adversary techniques of the courtroom. It really is best for the therapist to stay out of the courtroom scene, if possible.

There are other complications during this period, such as the paranoid husband who blames the therapist for misleading his wife into divorce proceedings and threatens legal suit against the therapist for such things as alienation of affection, malpractice, defamation of character. The litigious paranoid is notably a dangerous character in terms of potential murderous attempts against his imaginary enemies—sometimes even turning on his own lawyer. Therapists need to be aware of their own emotions during these trying periods and to deal judiciously with pressures from patients and lawyers.

When conjoint therapy is being used, the picture of the divorce period is obviously different. There is an opportunity here for the mates to decide mutually to end the relationship on mutually agreeable terms, and the mates and the therapist can work toward this goal. However, it is not surprising that often the conjoint therapy falls apart at this point. The best of intentions fail. When money issues are involved, the worst elements in people erupt. Again, often despite conjoint therapy, the lawyers take over the field, often with harm to one or both mates (Usdin, 1965).

In viewing the destructive aspects of divorce, one cannot avoid considering the harm done to children. Often in therapy of mates during divorce proceedings or after divorce, the main effort is to minimize the harm done to the children. The parent who is determined to resist the terms of the divorce to get back at the other mate uses the child to continue the fighting. Child support and visitation rights battles become areas in which marital therapists and child psychiatrists are brought into the battle. The legal question involved is whether courts should abdicate their responsibility with respect to visitation or support to either parent. Sometimes the marital therapist can have more positive influence on the potentially destructive parent than can legal recourse.

CREATIVE ASPECTS OF DIVORCE

In his book *Creative Divorce*: *A New Opportunity for Personal Growth*, divorce therapist Mel Krantzler (1973) outlines a process that goes from the death of the relationship through a period of mourning to an ultimate rebirth of the individual. The author's specialty was motivated by the break-up of his own twenty-four-year marriage.

He describes the step-by-step process in his own experiences with divorce and reports on experiences of others gathered in his divorce adjustment counseling. Even though these people had not been in therapy before the divorces, their problems are remarkably similar to what I have seen described in patients in treatment before divorce. Krantzler emphasizes the gratification of watching women develop inner resources that had been buried during their marriages and using them to create happy and fulfilling lives as single people. His personal experience with divorce resulted in the most personally enriching experience of his life.

Marital therapists should become knowledgeable in divorce therapy as a continuation of therapeutic services. As we have seen, patients

with marital problems often establish pathological interpersonal relations of a clinging infant to the mate. The mate can vary from one
extreme to another, along a continuum from clinging infant to individuated, adequate adult, to isolated automaton incapable of intimacy.
Those who fail to change cannot consider divorce as a solution or,
if they do divorce, immediately after or prior to the divorce are involved in another clinging relationship. If they cannot find one, they
become depressed. Those who succeed in changing can choose divorce
and can choose a period of being on their own and establishing their
separate identity. If they later form a new close relationship, it is of
a different nature. It is as one individual to another individual.

In summary, treatment of individuals involved in divorce as a solution to a disturbed marriage involves the problems of capacity for
separation, individuation, and maturation. Such treatment entails making a virtue of a necessity—using the unfortunate necessity for the
divorce to stimulate the discovery and the development of a unique,
separate individual.

Nontraditional Marital Patterns

Today we are faced with the complex social-psychological phenomenon of large numbers of people moving away from the traditional
marriage pattern of monogamy to the search for alternative lifestyles.
Although there has been controversy as to whether or not these
phenomena stem from the new sets of social and marital stresses unique
to the late twentieth century, history discounts the modern stress
theory (Lasch, 1973). Modern Americans are not the first to dispense
with wedded bliss; medieval Europeans had a variety of alternatives.
The society of Western Europe in the Middle Ages held marriage
in low repute and large numbers of people lived unmarried. Living
unmarried implied neither a life of solitude nor even celibacy.

The current increase in new marriage styles and fashions actually
has little direct clinical impact upon marital therapists, as shown by
the paucity of literature on psychotherapy of individuals involved in
these experiences. It would seem that individuals actively involved in
such styles do not often seek marital psychotherapy. Psychotherapy
is sought by the dropouts and failures from the newer styles.

One of the explanations of this complex phenomenon lies in the vicissitudes of values. Our recent society, characterized by the disintegration of values, has called for psychotherapy to help recover values (May, 1975). The wave of alternative lifestyles is a turning away from monogamy and psychotherapy in search of new values embedded in the new lifestyles which will fulfill the inner need for something new that will work. Reading the literature on "swinging," group marriage, open contracts, etc., reveals authors writing with what appears to be personal biases and a missionary zeal to find converts to new lifestyles (Smith and Smith, 1974).

Some of these movements seem to be less involved in attacking conventional forms of marriage, as they are interested in promoting a "humanistic" sexual freedom movement. In this way they are also interested in single persons and unmarried couples. "The focus is on consensual sexuality in general and consensual adultery in particular, the latter analyzed in terms of three forms of transmarital or transmonogamous sexuality: (1) adultery toleration, (2) co-marital sex, and (3) group marriage and communal cohabitation" (Smith and Smith, 1975).

The "open relationship" movements go beyond swinging. Swinging is largely recreational, allowing sexual involvement but minimal interpersonal or emotional depth. Swinging may contain its own set of rules, boundaries, and limitations. In fact, it can be a method intended to keep a jaded marriage together. Open relations, on the other hand, allow couples to maintain relationships with others on physical, emotional, and other levels. Crucial to this concept is the notion of freedom, the freedom of each partner to relate individually to others while living together in an intimate and loving relationship.

It is clear that this latter approach is not marriage oriented. It is individual-growth oriented, and if another primary partner is found, that is accepted as part of the growth process. The constantly recurring problem in such an approach is the problem of jealousy, and even when dealt with openly, it is never completely eliminated. One of the difficulties with practitioners of such lifestyles is that they tend to advocate it for everyone. They do not understand that even though some individuals might be able to succeed, at least during the period that they are out to prove their cause, others could not possibly tolerate such conditions. The United States may be moving toward acceptance of pluralistic lifestyles, but to try to impose a new one as the "right" one or the "only" one is indeed shortsighted.

One of the difficulties with zealots effecting social change and doing social engineering is that they do not understand that each set of conditions has advantages and disadvantages. When a new life style is effected to free one of the disadvantages of the old style, a new set of disadvantages that has to be dealt with will appear. The change that occurs is substituting a new set of disadvantages for the old ones and finding a new set of advantages to make up for those advantages which were lost from the old style. For example, to oversimplify the issues, the old-style monogamous marriage may have security accompanied by some sexual boredom. The new style open marriage may have sexual excitement accompanied by insecurity and jealousy. Everyone has a right to choose his or her own pleasures or poisons.

In doing therapy with people utilizing or advocating alternative lifestyles, the therapist must be especially aware of his personal value system and of his countertransference feelings. One of the difficulties I have noticed with such individuals is with the marriage-oriented therapist. If the patient is person-oriented and the therapist is marriage-oriented, there is an obvious incompatibility. The reverse of this is with the therapist who is personal-growth oriented and the patients who only claim to be. A basic incompatibility is obvious here too. Therapists are by training growth and development oriented. Patients naturally must overcome their own resistance to change, despite the inner pressures from their symptoms.

In summarizing, the main issue involved in monogamy or any alternate styles is whether the individual has the capacity to utilize it as a creative experience. If so, monogamy gives the potential for personal growth and development equal to any alternate style. To place the emphasis on the style in marriage is like placing the emphasis on the therapeutic technique used, rather than on the creativity in the patient and in the therapist.

Thinking that sex is the answer is nothing new. Freud early in his work also thought this. There is no one answer in the complex nature of the human being. Marital therapists observe the creative aspects of love, which is not coextensive with sex.

There is no such thing as an ideal style for marriage. "The ideal marriage is a snare, a trap, an image the worship of which destroys life. The ideal marriage is like the ideal body or any other ideal, useful only if it engenders the divine discontent which leads to questing and authenticity" (Jourard, 1975).

REFERENCES

Berman, E. M., and Lief, H. I. (1975), Marital therapy from a psychiatric perspective: an overview. *Amer. J. Psychiat.*, 132: 583-592.

Briscoe, C. W., and Smith, J. B. (1973), Depression and marital turmoil. *Archives of General Psychiatry*, 29: 811-817.

Cookerly, J. R. (1973), The outcome of the six major forms of marriage counseling compared: A pilot study. *Journal of Marriage and the Family*, 35, 4: 608-611.

Epstein, J. (1974), *Divorced in America.* New York: E. P. Dutton and Co.

Felder, R. L. (1971), *Divorce.* New York: World Publishing.

Hollender, M. H. (1959), Marriage and divorce. *Archives of General Psychiatry*, 1: 657-661.

Jourard, S. M. (1975), Marriage is for life. *Journal of Marriage and Family Counseling*, 1: 199-208.

Kantzler, M. (1973), *Creative Divorce.* New York: M. Evans.

Lasch, C. (1973), *The Columbia Forum*, 2: 4. New York: Columbia University.

May, R. (1975), Values, myths and symbols. *The American Journal of Psychiatry*, 132: 703-706.

Smith, J. R., and Smith, L. G. (1974), *Beyond Monogamy: Recent Studies of Sexual Alternatives in Marriage.* Baltimore: The Johns Hopkins University Press.

Smith, J. R., and Smith, L. G. (1975), *Consenting Adults: An Exploratory Study of the Sexual Freedom Movement.* In Press.

Sussman, M. (1972), *Non-Traditional Family Forms in the 1970's.* Minneapolis: National Counsel on Family Relations.

Usdin, G. L. (1965), Marital problems and the attorney. *Loyola Law Review*, 12, 2: 9-17.

Whitaker, C. A., and Miller, M. H. (1969), A reevaluation of "psychiatric help" when divorce impends. *Amer. J. Psychiat.*, 126: 611-622.

10

The Marital Therapist

THE TRAINING OF THE MARITAL THERAPIST

MARITAL THERAPISTS come from a wide variety of disciplines with wide variation in training, experience, ability, and goals. They can limit themselves to treating the least psychologically-shaken, consisting of persons unable to cope with aspects of their immediate marital situations which temporarily overtax their adaptive capacities (Frank, 1975). However, training requirements for treating this group should not be underestimated, since persons shaken by current life stresses can manifest the entire gamut of neurotic and psychotic symptoms (Tyhurst, 1957). Well-trained marital therapists are also called upon to treat couples made up of one or two mates who have psychoses that have genetic-organic determinants. Although psychotherapy cannot cure such psychoses, maintaining a harmonious marital relationship can significantly ameliorate the psychotic's distress and help him to function better. A well-trained marital therapist has available techniques capable of treating marital disorders per se, no matter how serious they are, or other serious disorders that have not responded to other threapies and are given additional relief by the adjunctive use of marital therapy.

An interesting illustrative study was done showing the interactions of drug therapy with marital therapy in depressive patients (Friedman,

1975). Using outpatient treatment of depressed patients (172 had neurotic or reactive depression; 15 had psychotic depressive reactions; 5 had manic-depressive psychoses, depressed phase; and 4 had involutional psychotic reactions), patients were assigned randomly to four treatment groups in a 2 x 2 factorial design. The four groups were: (1) drug-marital therapy; (2) drug-minimal contact; (3) placebo-marital therapy; and (4) placebo-minimal contact.

The active drug condition was found to be superior to its placebo control throughout the study. The drug effects were found to be superior to the marital therapy effects in regard to improvement in the patient's symptomatic and clinical condition (faster in achieving a significant advantage in four weeks). The marital therapy effects, however, were superior to the drug effects in regard to improvement in the patient's participation and performance in family role tasks and in perception of the spouse's attitude and behavior in the marriage. In regard to reducing hostility and enhancing the perception of the marital relationship, drug therapy produced a significantly better early effect which later decreased, while marital therapy, which did not affect hostility initially and which actually produced a negative initial effect on the patient's perception of the marital relationship, was superior to drug therapy in these two areas at the end of the course of treatment.

The marital therapy condition, compared to its minimal contact control condition, was found to effect significantly more symptom relief and clinical improvement. Some of this effect occurred as early as four weeks, and the positive results accumulated so that they were even greater in the end-point analysis.

For most of the outcome measures, the patient group that received both the active drug and marital therapy showed more improvement than any of the other three patient groups. This study showed that the simultaneous administration of active drug treatment and marital therapy in patients with reactive depression does not interfere with or cancel out the specific beneficial effects of each, but rather enhances these effects.

What is illustrated here is the importance of a breadth and depth of training for marital therapists so that such innovative approaches as the study cited above can place the major responsibility upon the therapist to be adaptable to the patient's needs. Everyone seems to be agreed, in theory at least, that there should be a pluralism in the education of the mental health professional. From this basic agreement in thought, though often not achieved in practice, a wide divergence of conclusions are drawn. At one extreme (the direction which I favor) is training the individual to be knowledgeable and capable of using any of several schools of thought. As presented by Havens (1973), the direction is to move psychiatry from the sectarianism that grips it toward science and a more effective practice. When applied to the field of marital therapy, it places the burden on the therapist to be knowledgeable and skilled in the many approaches presented in this book and new ones to come. This is obviously idealistic and perhaps not obtainable, but the direction is desirable.

In contrast, a practical conclusion is Jerome Frank's emphasis on pluralism in the education of the mental health professional so that the trainee can make a rational choice to concentrate on an approach "congenial to his own personality" (Frank, 1975). This puts the responsibility on the patient to find that type of therapy and therapist which will be congenial to his personality. Or, in a university or clinic setting where there are groups of therapists using different approaches, it might be possible for a triage system to refer that type of patient who could best use a particular approach of one of the available groups of therapists. This would not work well with the individual therapist in private practice. For this therapist, intensive and extensive training and flexibility would offer the greatest opportunity for his patients.

Since there are but a few well-rounded training centers in the United States, and since the state of training marital therapists is an amorphous one (Nichols, 1974), the responsibility for the degree of training is placed squarely on the shoulders of the individual therapist. Unfortunately, the trend seems to be away from intensive advanced training. Personal psychotherapy for all psychotherapists, marital or otherwise, formerly considered to be the cornerstone of doing psychotherapy, is losing favor and opportunities to learn and grow are thus being missed. In psychiatry residency training, with the abolishment of a preliminary year of the general rotating internship, opportunities to grow and learn are being missed. In a discipline where the patient's growth and learning are the *modus operandi* of the treatment, it seems contradictory that the therapist does not always practice what he teaches.

In fact, there is no such thing as completion of training. Involvement in forms of marital therapy where another therapist is involved, whether it be collaborative, conjoint, or combined, with more than one therapist or group, is a form of continuous supervision and training. I also use observation of myself doing marital therapy by trainees and staff as a form of continuing supervision and training. The following material both illustrates this point and demonstrates the problem of countertransference in marital therapy (Bird and Martin, 1956).

COUNTERTRANSFERENCE IN MARITAL THERAPY

The following case is an example of the collaborative form (stereoscopic technique) of treating marital disharmony. It is extremely condensed.

Clinical Material

The clinical data have been extracted from the concurrent therapies of a middle-aged husband and wife, both of whom suffered from severe psychiatric disorders. Work with this couple began after the family physician recognized that it would become necessary to hospitalize the wife if psychotherapy were not instituted promptly. Since he was unable to persuade the wife to seek the needed help, he advised the husband to consult a psychiatrist first, in the hope that she would later follow suit. This device met with success when the wife usurped the husband's fourth appointment. During her third hour, she insisted that she remain in treatment with the first psychiatrist and that her husband be referred to another psychiatrist.

Initial Stages of Therapy

During the early phase of the wife's treatment, she did little more than criticize her spouse. She complained that he did not love her, that he treated her as his social inferior, and that he wanted to be free of her. She placed little emphasis on her own emotional problems, which she summarized as a tendency to be "inadequate" when forced by the husband's defections to assume unwarranted responsibilities.

The husband entered treatment with no protest at having been sent away to a second psychiatrist. He quietly accepted the blame the wife had heaped upon him but denied her charges that he did not love her. He said that he wanted to cooperate fully with the therapist and to find out what in his childhood had caused his present difficulties. The opening hours of the treatment were filled with fantasies about an idyllic love relationship with his wife, free from strife but also free from physical contact.

In one of the initial therapists' conferences between the two psychiatrists, the wife's therapist presented his reconstructed version of the incident wherein she had an affair with a close friend, allegedly at the husband's instigation. This was offered as evidence of his rejecting attitude toward her and his inability to act the role of a man. The husband's psychiatrist reacted with skepticism and with sympathy for his patient. He expressed the opinion that the husband had been cuckolded, in view of the fact that the husband had become enraged when he heard about the incident and had retaliated by revealing to his wife for the first time an earlier affair of his own. On this occasion, the stereoscopic technique not only demonstrated its usefulness in detecting a distortion of reality—the falseness of the wife's accusation—but also brought to light what was later recognized to be a positive countertransference reaction to their respective patients on the part of both psychiatrists which clouded their objectivity.

Clarification of the Personality Structures of the Marriage Partners

During the next phase of the wife's treatment, the complaint that her husband did not love her recurred constantly. She made only passing references to the fact that she engaged in drinking bouts and outbursts of rage, and to her inadequacy in domestic and social situations. As memories of her childhood emerged, it became evident that her early life experiences were characterized by an intense fear of being alone and by an exaggerated need to depend on the adults in her home. As a terrified little girl, she had insisted on sleeping on a cot in the dining room where she would listen intently to family conversations in the adjoining parlor. When finally she was unable to tolerate her loneliness any longer, she would cry out and thus bring her father to her side. She then customarily demanded that he carry her tenderly upstairs.

An incident of repetition of this scene took place during this phase of the wife's therapy. Late one afternoon the husband urgently summoned her psychiatrist to their home, where the wife was found to be completely inebriated, disheveled, and furious with her husband, who fled the scene as soon as he admitted the physician to the house. The patient's attitude was so violent that the physician too became frightened.

During this phase of the husband's therapy, he continued to take full blame for his wife's problems and to protest that he loved her. Psychodynamically relevant material brought into focus a poignant picture of his choldhood. As a boy, he had been saddled with the responsibility for the care of a mentally defective younger brother. Their mother had refused to act on the recommendation that this child be institutionalized. The patient was both terrified and humiliated by his brother's violent outbursts and frequent episodes of soiling. But he continued to do his "duty."

In the therapists' meetings which dealt with the foregoing material, the wife's psychiatrist presented his reconstructed version of the episode of rage which he had witnessed in the patient's home. He concluded that her anger represented intense jealousy toward the daughter who, in the first place, was now the center of the family's attention and whose marriage, in addition, promised to provide the daughter with the love that the patient unrealistically felt she was not receiving from her husband. The colleague's version was somewhat different. He postulated that such rages were not uncommon and that they recurred as often as several times a week. He also concluded that the wife was not acknowledging her spouse's constant protection and his acceptance of her uncontrollable outbursts, and that indeed her therapist had been forced into repeating the role of the father in childhood and of the husband throughout the marriage.

After the husband's therapist had repeatedly heard his colleague place what seemed to be a disproportionate emphasis on the wife's "need to be loved," he made two discerning observations. He commented that the wife's psychiatrist not only had "fallen for the pink goddess line," but also was overlooking the fact that the wife needed to become more adequate. This confrontation placed the responsibility squarely on the wife's therapist to investigate and eliminate the blind spots he had developed. His subsequent self-analysis disclosed a negative countertransference attitude toward the wife, which he had until then denied. In reality, the psychiatrist feared and hence disliked her, a destructive woman, but he had defended himself against these feelings through the device of overvaluing and overprotecting her. As a consequence, he had been led into establishing the same kind of relationship with her as had existed between her and her father, the first person to be controlled by the "pink goddess." It was then evident that, so long as she could maintain her omnipotent defense against the recognition of her inadequacy, hostility, and dependence, no progress could be made.

In the course of the stereoscopic meetings which dealt with this material, the wife's psychiatrist at first expressed positive feelings for his patient and stressed her need for understanding and affection. However, somewhat later he confided to his colleague that she had proved to be a frustrating patient and that it had become a chore to work with her. In general, his comments took on a note of angry desperation, and he concluded them on one occasion by saying that he would go on with the patient because "there just isn't anything else I can do." He reminded the other psychiatrist that the referring physician had called the patient a "pathological liar" and remarked that the term was most appropriate for one who so blithely continued to project and distort reality. He reported that he had inexplicably cut one of her hours short by ten minutes and had subsequently felt guilty at having done this to a deprived person who needed love and consideration.

Once her therapist had dealt with his negative countertransference, his need to support her powerful defense no longer existed. With the lifting of this defense, work with the underlying impulses proceeded. As a result, the wife took some forward steps. She enlarged the scope of her activities and her circle of friends and came to demand less of her husband and more of herself.

During the regular meetings of the psychiatrists, the husband's therapist at the outset felt, in relating this material, sympathy for a man who was so burdened by a near-psychotic partner. But, as time wore on and the husband continued to present the same material in the same manner, his psychiatrist's reports carried a different tone. These later comments implied that it was difficult and unrewarding to work with such a passive male, a man who continued to be sexually impotent, who rarely got to work on time, and who drank as much as he ever did. The physician went on to emphasize that the patient strove mainly to play the role of the good little boy in the treatment hours, while running away from masculine responsibilities in his daily life. In connection with the fact that the patient sometimes clowned in the company of his friends, who then bought him drinks, the psychiatrist derisively likened him to Little Tommy Tucker, who "sang for his supper." In further observations, the psychiatrist stressed the difficulty of inducing the patient to face the perfectly obvious fact that his activities resulted from fear of and anger toward his wife. The psychiatrist finally insisted that the prognosis was very poor.

As the wife's psychiatrist listened to his colleague's reports in one of their meetings, it occurred to him to remind his associate that he himself had been frightened by the wife during the visit to the couple's home. After the reality of the wife's violent nature had been re-emphasized in this manner, the question was then raised as to why the husband's therapist had lost sight of this reality. It became apparent almost immediately that his vision had been obscured by strong negative countertransference feelings. When he was thus confronted by his own reaction, he did a piece of self-analysis which forced him to become aware of his derisive feelings toward a passive male who allows a woman to run him ragged and who, in this specific instance, was not dealing with the problem of his castration anxiety as the psychiatrist himself had done earlier in his own personal analysis. Once this understanding had been reached by the husband's therapist, a change in the therapeutic milieu ensued. It became easier for the psychiatrist to sit patiently through the succeeding hours and to bend his efforts to help the husband with his problem. In the course of time, the patient was able to express openly the repressed hostility toward his wife and made progress in working out the castration anxiety reinforced by her violence. For our purposes here it will suffice to say that the patient thereafter became more openly aggressive, and that he regained his potency with his wife.

The above material shows (1) the interference in psychotherapy of countertransference reactions, (2) the advantages of having one's psychotherapy supervised by a colleague, and (3) the advantages to the therapist of personal psychotherapy so that he can do bits of self-analysis as dictated by countertransference responses.

It might also be noted that this case is an unusually clear illustration of the dovetailing of neuroses between husband and wife.

The insight provided by the stereoscopic approach was utilized by the psychiatrists in identifying the pattern of this marriage. The husband's neurosis contained a repetition compulsion in which he re-created with his wife his martyrdom of caring for the uncontrolled defective brother. His wife's inadequacy, inability to control her violent feelings, and great need for attention certainly strengthened his unconscious identification of her with the brother. The wife was likewise driven by a repetition compulsion, specifically to maintain her infantile wish to be the "pink goddess" who would be loved unconditionally and on demand by her husband, as she had been by her father. Fascinatingly enough, in her dreams, the wife showed that she had identified herself with the husband's brother. For both partners, thus, the pink goddess and the retarded brother had become fused into a single image. As a consequence, an unconscious vicious circle was set in motion, in which the wife's identification with the frightening and demanding brother forced the husband to adopt the role of an overpassive, martyred "good boy." This interlocking of unconscious need had been the bond that for many years held together a destructive, disturbed marriage.

To return to our focus on countertransference, it is an acknowledged fact that countertransference feelings of the therapist can modify the therapeutic process. Any factor that interferes with the therapist's recognition of his countertransference constitutes a handicap, since a recognized countertransference reaction can become an adjunct to psychotherapy. The psychotherapist who finds himself unaccountably annoyed, frightened, or exhilarated by a particular patient has in his possession a diagnostic tool. If he will discover the origins of the countertransference reaction, he may find that his patient's unconscious is identical with that of a significant person in his own past. This knowledge can profitably be utilized in formulating or modifying the treatment program. In addition, the therapist who is capable of controlling or eliminating countertransference attitudes facilitates the therapeutic process. It has been conclusively demonstrated that the transference is a most valuable therapeutic tool, and nothing so impedes the development of the clear-cut, pertinent transference reaction in the patient as a negative countertransference reaction on the therapist's part.

The most significant development in the therapies of the couple under consideration was the reduction of the negative countertransference reactions, and their replacement by positive countertransferences which facilitated the husband's work with the problem of his castration anxiety and the wife's recognition of her hostile impulses and dependent strivings. It is our belief that use of the stereoscopic technique brought on this chain of events.

EMPATHY IN THE MARITAL THERAPIST

A great deal has been written about empathy and the therapist's capacity for empathy as a major therapeutic tool (Greenson, 1967). I will touch upon it briefly in order to be able to discuss empathy in marital therapy. Recognition is given to the fact that empathy can be conducive to therapy or can present hazards and be detrimental to therapy.

Shapiro (1974) offers a useful spectrum of five possible human experiences, ranging from highly egocentric to highly object-centered. (1) An individual may not acknowledge perceiving another's feelings. This response is clearly not empathic. (2) He may perceive another's feelings without understanding how they can occur. This response is also nonempathic. (3) He may perceive another's feelings and recognize that he feels or would feel similarly and that a specific circumstance is the basis of the congruence of feelings—a clearly empathic response, since it is based on the conviction that, given like circumstances, most people would feel the same way. (4) He may recognize that he feels as another does by observing him, without being aware of the causative agent—an experience of great immediacy, with intactness of ego boundaries between subject and observer. (5) He is convinced that he feels the same as another, regardless of the object's circumstance or expression—a loss of boundaries between self and object, with a conviction of merged experience.

The effectiveness of therapy is enhanced when the therapist maintains the third state above (empathy)—that is, there is transient identification in which the therapist preserves his separateness, as opposed to identification in which even the patient's feelings of helplessness are shared (Beres and Arlow, 1974). The therapist needs to be able to feel *with* the patient through identification, but he then should separate from him in order to feel *about* him.

Beres and Arlow (1974) make the important recognition that what the therapist shares with the patient in empathy is not only affect, but also cognition. The affect experienced by the therapist should not only tell how the patient feels but also how he wants the therapist to feel. If the therapist does not recognize the nature of the affects, countertransference that will impede therapy occurs rather than empathy.

It is a common clinical experience that when a therapist feels what the patient feels and communicates this to the patient, a very positive response is elicited. When to this is added an interpretation of how the patient is using this feeling to avoid change, a negative response is elicited. The patient commonly prefers an experience of feeling a merging of therapist and patient (which can present hazards and be detrimental to therapy) to the truly empathic state of a transient identification in which the therapist preserves his separateness. In this way, patients tend to prefer that the therapist's empathic processes suffer distortion and often attempt to effect in therapy a state in which therapist and patient reinforce empathic distortions in each other. A transient *folie à deux* can occur during therapy which is temporarily pleasurable to both therapist and patient. Thus, because empathy is so vulnerable to distortion, it must be carefully evaluated and monitored. The distinction between empathy and countertransference must be clearly made.

Marital therapy brings both the value and the dangers of empathy into sharp relief. When both mates are seen in conjoint types of therapy, the ideal of simultaneous empathic responses to both partners, who are in opposition to one another, is difficult to attain. What usually occurs is a shifting from one to the other with varying lengths of elapsed time. Distortions of empathy in the marital therapist in the direction of one mate are quickly reacted against by the other. This acts as a type of supervision for the therapist. Thus, in conjoint marital therapy there is less likelihood of therapist and patient reinforcing empathic distortions than in dyadic therapy. When mutual reinforcement of distortions of empathy does occur in marital therapy, it becomes a serious impediment to the therapy.

Empathic responses in the therapist in marital therapy are essential, but empathy is not enough. Interpretation and insight into the nature of each individual's dynamics and of the interpersonal relationship within the context of the family setting are intertwining forces leading to therapeutic effectiveness in marital therapy.

THE PERSON IN THE MARITAL THERAPIST

I wish to complete this chapter and this book with a simple message. It is that the marital therapist has a remarkable opportunity for personal growth and development. The opportunities presented in working with marital couples allow the therapist a deeper and broader understanding of the experiences in his original family and a chance for continuing change and growth in his immediate family. It is an exciting experience to observe either how initial creative changes within patient couples stimulate creative changes within marital therapists or how creative changes within the marital therapists stimulate creative changes within the patient couples.

The following is a brief example of this observation but it also illustrates the important difference between first-order change, which (though an opposite response) in effect means no change at all, and a second-order creative change, which is problem solving (Watzlawick, et al., 1974).

This patient couple in a marital couples group presented a common complaint by the wife that her husband did not pay attention to her. He was a very gregarious person who invited foreign dignitaries to their home for dinner. During dinner he spent all of his time talking, with obvious interest and pleasure, to the guests. To make matters worse, they spoke in the visitors' native tongue, which she did not understand. As she ventilated her unhappiness to the group, they told her that she was too passive and that she must change. She was told that she must speak up and tell him to stop it. The wife responded to their suggestions by speaking up to her husband and threatening never to make another dinner if he did not change. He reacted by inviting more friends, continuing to speak in the visitors' foreign language, and arranging for the dinner to be catered by a gourmet cook. Her next choice if she continued in her new direction of not being so passive was not to attend the dinners.

At this point she made a creative leap, a second-order change, beyond the group and the marital therapists. She set about learning the foreign language and using her own gourmet cooking talents. She started to enjoy the opportunity to meet interesting people, to speak in their native tongue, and to grow the person within her. It need hardly be noted that the process of psychological separation from the husband, and individuation, had begun. Beyond the shocking experience to the married couples group was the effect it had upon the marital therapists. One of the therapists "incidentally" started to learn to read and speak the native tongue of his parents which he had resisted doing since childhood. The other therapist, who had a reputation as being a horrible cook, took a trip to a gourmet cooking school in London, from which she returned refreshed and exuberant. It is clear that both marital therapists were listening to this woman in a healthy manner —with open minds. Such effective listening can have great curative value, leading to new insights and awareness (Barbara, 1973).

The principal requirement for a marital therapist is the creative capacity to continuously grow and develop as a person and, through this, to offer a milieu in which the patients have the greatest opportunity for change.

REFERENCES

Barbara, D. A. (1973), Healthy and neurotic aspects of listening. *American Journal of Psychoanalysis*, 33: 185-192.
Beres, D., and Arlow, J. A. (1974), Fantasy and identification in empathy. *Psychoanalytic Quarterly*, 43: 26-50.

Bird, H. W., and Martin, P. A. (1956), Countertransference in the psychotherapy of marriage partners. *Psychiatry*, 19: 353-360.

Frank, J. D. (1975), An overview of psychotherapy. In *Overview of the Psychotherapies*, ed. G. Usdin. New York: Brunner/Mazel.

Friedman, A. S. (1975), Interaction of drug therapy with marital therapy in depressive patients. *Archives of General Psychiatry*, 32: 619-637.

Greenson, R. R. (1967), *The Technique and Practice of Psychoanalysis*. New York: International Universities Press.

Havens, L. L. (1973), *Approaches to the Mind*. Boston: Little, Brown and Company.

Nichols, W. C., Jr. (1974), Editor, *Marriage and Family Therapy*. Section 7: Preparation and training of marriage counselors. Minneapolis: National Council on Family Relations.

Shapiro, J. (1974), The development and distortions of empathy. *Psychoanalytic Quarterly*, 43: 4-25.

Tyhurst, J. S. (1957), The role of transition states—including disasters—in mental illness. In *Symposium on Preventive and Social Psychiatry*. Washington, D. C.: Walter Reed Army Institute of Research.

Watzlawick, P., Weakland, J., and Fisch, R. (1974), *Change: Principles of Problem Formation and Problem Resolution*. New York: W. W. Norton and Co., Inc.

Whitaker, C. A., Felder, R. E., and Warkentin, J. (1965), Countertransference in the family treatment of schizophrenia. In *Intensive Family Therapy*, ed. I. Boszormenyi-Nagy and J. L. Framo. New York: Harper and Row.

INDEX

Index